Invest in Penny Stocks

A GUIDE TO PROFITABLE TRADING

Peter Leeds

WILEY

John Wiley & Sons, Inc.

Published by John Wiley & Sons, Inc., Hoboken, New Jersey.
Published simultaneously in Canada.

For general information on our other products and services or for technical support, please contact our Customer Care Department within the United States at (800) 762-2974, outside the United States at (317) 572-3993 or fax (317) 572-4002.

Wiley also publishes its books in a variety of electronic formats. Some content that appears in print may not be available in electronic books. For more information about Wiley products, visit our web site at www.wiley.com.

Library of Congress Cataloging-in-Publication Data:

Leeds, Peter.
    Invest in penny stocks : a guide to profitable trading / Peter Leeds.
        p. cm.
    Includes index.
    ISBN 978-0-470-93218-6 (cloth);   ISBN 978-1-118-01327-4 (ebk);
        ISBN 978-1-118-01328-1 (ebk);   ISBN 978-1-118-01329-8 (ebk)
        1. Penny stocks.   2. Investments.   I. Title.
    HG6041.L443 2011
    332.63'22–dc22

                                                                            2010042168

Printed in the United States of America
10 9 8 7 6 5 4 3 2 1

For my wife—
a heroic woman whose patience and wisdom
are without equal.

Contents

Contents

Preface

"Most of the greatest stocks started small."

—Peter Leeds

Imagine a company that was debt free, was extremely profitable, and owned an incredible new technology.

What if that investment was trading for pennies? You could invest a small amount, and walk away with a small fortune.

Would you be able to find that company? Thanks to *Invest in Penny Stocks*, now you will.

Let me take you on a journey into the world of high-flying penny stocks. Come with me as I walk through every aspect of these exciting investments, from the very beginning.

You will learn:

- How to find the highest quality penny stocks
- Which penny stocks to avoid
- How to trade risk-free
- The best buying prices
- When to take profits

I'll also introduce you to Leeds Analysis. This system allows you to find penny stocks that are about to jump up in price, and helps you get involved before the rest of the investment world.

I've also included many of my favorite Trading Tactics, which could supercharge your investing results just as they have for me.

The appetite for penny stocks is higher than it's ever been. Unfortunately, most people are buying the wrong shares and at the wrong prices. I've written this book to help you invest in penny stocks the right way.

Have fun, and at any point feel free to get in touch with me directly. I can't wait to hear your success stories.

Best wishes,

Peter Leeds
The Penny Stock Professional
www.PeterLeeds.com
1.866.My.Leeds (1.866.695.3337)

Experience Level
Rating System (EL)

Invest in Penny Stocks is meant to be a simplified, easy-to-understand book that explains a wide range of topics of varying complexity.

Given the various degrees of skill level of the readership, not all concepts need to be read by everyone. An experienced trader already knows the difference between market and limit orders, whereas that section will be very significant for new investors.

More experienced investors may want to skip some of the simpler sections if they already have an understanding of the topic.

Newer investors may want to leave the more complex sections for last, until they've gotten a grasp of the less-advanced supporting ideas.

Experience Level 1: There is no complexity or difficulty to these sections at all.

Experience Level 2: Even brand-new investors will have no trouble with these ideas.

Experience Level 3: These are very beneficial concepts that are not difficult to understand.

Experience Level Rating System (EL)

Experience Level 4: Even experienced traders will benefit from these sections.

Experience Level 5: These are the most complicated sections.

1

The Big Business of Penny Stocks

PENNY STOCKS ARE BIG BUSINESS

**Experience
Level I**
●●●●

They may sound small, but penny stocks are big business. The phrase "penny stocks" is one of the most popular financial searches on the Internet. In fact, it gets more searches than terms like "stock picks," "stock quotes," "New York Stock Exchange," or "stock broker."

This translates into tens of millions of investors in America, and millions more worldwide, actively searching for information and guidance on penny stocks. Unfortunately, hidden motivations abound, and misinformation outweighs the amount of proper analysis. As the Penny Stock Professional, I am actively working to change this state of affairs.

My team and I help people avoid some of the common dangers, and find the best penny stock companies with the greatest upside. You'll find that it is quite simple—it's extremely lucrative to get involved with the best 5 percent of penny stocks. These companies will have:

- Strong management teams
- Good upside potential
- Proven revenues

- Patented technologies
- Solid financial trends

Finding and investing in the best penny stocks is one of the most lucrative ways to make money on the stock market, or to make money at anything for that matter.

Broad Appeal of Penny Stocks

I love the broad appeal of penny stocks. Unlike most investment vehicles, which get the attention only of specific types of people, penny stocks seem to generate interest among all types of investors, of all skill levels and all financial situations.

If you are a beginner, you'll learn about trading quite quickly, because penny stocks move faster and are more volatile than more conventional investments. Your learning curve will be much shorter than if you just put money into IBM and let it sit there for a year or two.

If you have limited funds to invest, penny stocks give you the potential of actually making something out of your money. A $1,000 investment can multiply many times over, compared to putting that cash into a slow-moving blue chip or a super-safe bond, even if you let it sit there for years and years.

If you are an experienced trader, penny stocks are appropriate for a portion of your portfolio because they add excitement and big-gain potential to your investments.

If you know what to look for, and thus get involved with really high-quality companies, it can translate into massive gains. So many of these high-quality penny stocks are trading for pennies a share simply because they are:

- Overlooked
- Undiscovered
- Unfairly valued
- Sold off in sympathy with a sector or the overall market

Look, I've been involved with investing from all angles, and still am, including:

- Real estate
- Derivatives/options
- Penny stocks
- Large-cap stocks

Based on extensive personal experience, and the many years of analysis/research/editing I've done at PeterLeeds.com, I've come to the rock-solid conclusion that:

Penny stocks are the most lucrative and realistic method for building wealth that I've encountered.

With penny stocks, gains come more rapidly and the returns are greater. What's the point of putting $500 on some massive company, and a year later you've made 10 or 15 percent on your money? And that's considered a good return? *Hello, 45 bucks*—big deal!

All you've done is tied up your money for a year to make an insignificant profit (or maybe even took a loss) and given up the opportunity to have that $500 potentially do something more. Maybe something *much* more.

Especially if you have a small portfolio, the gains you will probably get from blue-chip stocks are going to seem insignificant. They aren't going to change your life. There's no excitement in it.

Yet people are afraid of penny stocks, and might argue that blue-chip stocks, like GM and IBM and Exxon, are better investments because they're based on better companies. Yes, blue chips are a lot better than 95 percent of the penny stocks out there. However, in terms of upside potential, growth of your investment, and life-changing profits, the 5 percent of penny stocks that make the Leeds Analysis cut represent far more compelling investments, and very often are far superior companies. They're just smaller. Much smaller. And the best part is once you find these high-quality penny stocks, you get to pick them up for pennies a share!

As the Penny Stock Professional, my job is to help steer you toward the 5 percent of penny stocks that may dramatically outperform every other investment option that's out there, including so-called "safe" blue chips.

 The 5 Percent Rule

Only about 5 percent of penny stocks pass Leeds Analysis. Those that pass the test are:

- Significantly more likely to outperform the rest
- Fundamentally very strong
- Less likely to suffer downside price moves
- More likely to enjoy massive upside potential

Some of the criteria we look for with Leeds Analysis include, but are not limited to:

- Strong management teams
- A track record of gains in revenues
- Accelerating increases in earnings
- High barriers to entry to the industry
- Company approaching profitability or already profitable
- Low or no debt load
- Patented technologies and/or strong intellectual property rights
- Involvement in a growing industry or market
- Strong and long-term competitive advantages
- Superior and effective branding, positioning, and marketing

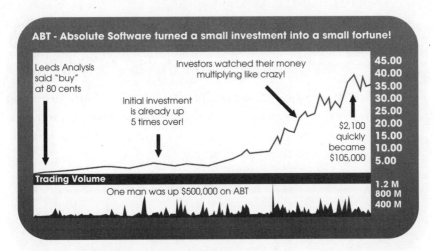

Figure 1.1   Absolute Software Trading

Subscribers to Peter Leeds may remember some of the homeruns we've hit using Leeds Analysis, like Absolute Software, which went from $0.80 to $40.64! (split adjusted). (See Figure 1.1.)

Another great example, Disc Inc., spiked from only $0.38 per share all the way up to $9.93 for a 2,500 percent gain! (See Figure 1.2.)

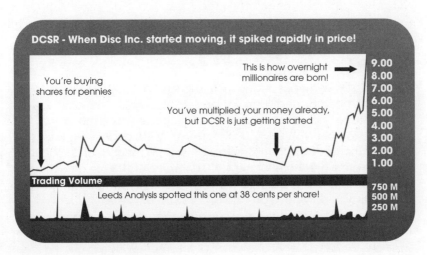

Figure 1.2   Disc Inc. Trading

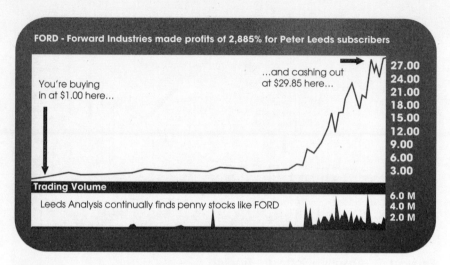

Figure 1.3   Forward Industries Trading

Or take Forward Industries, which we revealed to Peter Leeds subscribers when it was trading at $1.00, before it absolutely exploded to $29.85 for a total gain of 2,885 percent! (See Figure 1.3.)

You wouldn't see gains like that in IBM or Exxon even if you waited a lifetime!

Trading Tactics: Averaging Down

Averaging down means buying more shares of a stock you already own if the price has dropped since you originally bought it. This tactic lowers your average price paid per share, but increases your exposure.

For example, you buy 2,000 shares at $2.00, and weeks later the stock drops to $1.00. If you buy another 2,000 shares at $1.00, your average price per share for the 4,000 units is now $1.50. In other words, if the shares make it back to $1.50, you are breaking even overall. (However, you now have an additional $2,000 invested.)

I have personally seen people average all the way down, with three or four or five new buy orders over months or years. They lost their shirts on stocks like Nortel and some of the Internet high-flyers.

Trading Tactics: Averaging Down *(Continued)*

Investors usually average down to make up for a bad trading decision. This can get pretty ugly when a stock is nose-diving toward zero, as they throw good money after bad.

I don't support the concept of averaging down. In fact, if you abide by the methodology of *limiting losses* that we describe later, you won't be in a position where you'd need to average down, because you already would have jumped from that sinking ship.

Bad investors average down, buying more shares of a falling stock to decrease the average price per share they've paid. This strategy is hardly ever effective. In addition, it magnifies your losses if the stock keeps dropping. Nevertheless, individual investors seem to continually engage in this practice.

When I trade, I'm much more likely to *average up*. I'll acquire more shares as the stock price climbs and the momentum of the company rises. The increasing share price is a confirmation of the success of my original analysis, and the company's progress, rather than a profit-taking opportunity.

Penny Stock Phobia

People have a phobia of penny stocks. This fear has been instilled in them because they hear a lot of bad stories about people who have been "swindled," "ripped off," or otherwise "scammed." Other people may have had personal experiences, or heard stories of others that ended with lost money.

These may have been real experiences, and real stories, and that doesn't surprise me at all. I am telling you that **most people who trade penny stocks lose money.** This is almost always because they invest:

- For the wrong reasons
- At the wrong time
- (Most notably) in the wrong companies

For every nine people losing $1 on the market, the tenth person is making $9. That tenth person could be you, if you learn to invest:

- For the right reasons
- At the right time
- (Most notably) in the right companies

This book, with its explanation of Leeds Analysis, will help you do that. Not everyone is successful with it, and penny stocks can go up or down in price. However, I do have a track record of people whom I don't even know, who've never met me, sending me pictures of boats and cars and other things they bought with money they made trading penny stocks based on my guidance.

Some of these people have followed my picks at my online newsletter, *Peter Leeds Penny Stocks*. Others have read my earlier book, *Understanding Penny Stocks*. However they came to their penny stock successes, each one of them proves even more that Leeds Analysis works and can give investors of all experience levels, and from all walks of life, an unfair financial advantage.

Penny Stocks May Not Be for You

Penny stocks might not be an appropriate investment vehicle for you, based on your experience level, risk tolerance, or personal investment strategy.

It's important that you know when *not* to trade penny stocks:

- You're losing sleep at night because you're stressed out.
- You wind up fighting with your spouse about it.
- You think about it so much that you aren't paying attention to your family.
- Your mind wanders while you're at work.

If you find yourself thinking about your penny stock investments too frequently, this type of investing may not be right for you. Of course, this doesn't apply to plain excitement, when your penny stocks are multiplying in value and your constant thoughts are positive ones. Rather, it's when negative associations start cropping up that you may want to take a break from the world of low-priced shares.

It is also important to have realistic expectations. A lot of less-experienced investors think they can turn $1,000 into a million bucks just by trading penny stocks. Many people have great success stories and make a lot of money, but it's not realistic to expect to make such ridiculous amounts.

Yes, technically, it is possible. It has happened. Of course, those are extremely rare situations. That will not happen to you. If you prove me wrong, that's fantastic, but it is not helpful to expect such a monumental degree of success. It's important that you have realistic expectations.

Penny stocks go up in value very frequently, doubling or tripling in price. Very often penny stocks go down in price. You need to have a good comprehension of this. Don't enter the penny stock arena until you're ready to approach it with a sensible understanding.

You should get involved with penny stocks only with risk money, especially at first and certainly if you're a less experienced trader. Don't put money into penny stocks that you need for your children's education, or your retirement, or your mortgage. In other words, never put your grocery money into the stock market.

Should you talk to your financial planner? Absolutely. You could talk to them about penny stocks, but I'll save you the trip. I'll tell you what they'll say:

- "No, it's dangerous."
- "It's ridiculous."
- "Stay away from penny stocks."

Hey, I actually happen to agree with them! Penny stocks are dangerous, and ridiculous, and you *should* stay away from them. Most penny stocks will potentially cost you money. In that sense, I agree with the doom-saying financial planners.

Where I diverge from their generalized opinion is as follows: Once you know how to find the 5 percent of penny stocks that represent high-quality investments, penny stock investing becomes possibly the most lucrative way to build wealth.

I Do Not Give Advice

Understand that anything you read or hear from me is not advice. I don't give advice. I don't know you. I don't know your trading style, your financial situation, or your time outlook (long term, short term, day trader). I can't know what kind of stock is best for you or what you should do with your money. I don't know the answers to these things, nor do I want to know.

I can't talk to you about what's best for your retirement, or what you should do with your savings, or how to make your money double the fastest. I'm just going to give you opinions and guidance, based on my experience and the results of Leeds Analysis. After that, it all comes down to your deciding what's best for you. At the end of the day you need to take responsibility for your trading decisions, regardless of where your stock picks first originated.

We've had subscribers at Peter Leeds Penny Stocks who have come to us complaining that they lost money on a stock pick we made. At the same time we have had subscribers who are providing testimonials because they are making money on that exact same stock in the same time period! Some people just traded it better than others. Your own personal skill level and trading strategy will come into play.

Over the years, the Peter Leeds Penny Stocks subscribers who have fared the best (by far) were the ones that used my research and analysis as one part of a more balanced, overall trading strategy. If we made a stock selection that they didn't love, they would pass and wait for a different pick. If we made a stock selection that appealed to them, they would look into it more deeply, and decide for themselves if it fit their trading style and investment goals.

In *Invest in Penny Stocks*, I'm not going to go into very much detail about how trading works and how the stock markets work. All of that information is available in my other book, *Understanding Penny Stocks*. I will merely touch on some general topics very briefly when I feel the need for a general explanation.

Mainly, I will focus on the more highly advanced techniques that have the potential to make you (or save you) a lot of money. These strategies have been very effective for me, and were developed over many years through trial and error as well as in the trenches with millions in live money.

From the defensive side, you're going to learn how to avoid the duds and dangers that are out there in the penny stock world. As well, you need to avoid the scams that you may encounter.

Then we're going to get into some really fun stuff. I'll explain the techniques that I use to turn penny stock theory into actual cash profits. From "Leeds Analysis" to "Trading Windows," from "Scaling In" to "Volatility Plays," I haven't held anything back.

So, let's get started!

Experience Level 3

Trading Tactics: Buy the Rumor, Sell the Fact

There is an expression in the stock market that says, "Buy the rumor, sell the fact." It's a lesson that all new traders should learn, because it will help them profit while avoiding selling too late.

The idea is simple. When there's an outstanding rumor about an upcoming event for a company, investors buy in once they hear about it through the grapevine, thus pushing share prices higher. Once the event itself is actually realized, the share price loses that upward buying pressure and the stock drops in value.

For example, ABC Inc. is likely to get FDA approval for its new drug. The upcoming ruling is widely expected, and many investors buy in,

(Continued)

Trading Tactics: Buy the Rumor, Sell the Fact
(*Continued*)

speculating that the announcement will send the shares skyward. This starts pushing the stock upward.

Eventually, once the actual FDA approval comes out, the shares don't spike much higher since the speculators had already run the share price up so much. Now that the announcement is out, many of those same speculators start cashing out, putting a great deal of selling pressure on the stock. Thus, despite the release of some very positive news, the shares actually head lower!

Examples of What Might Drive Buying Interest

- Impending patent award
- Potential dismissal of major lawsuit against the company
- Expected strong financial results
- New major customer or contract win widely anticipated
- Upcoming release of a new version of the company's technology
- Anticipated FDA clearance

Any such widely known and expected event would gradually push share prices higher. This would have steam until, and only until, the expected event itself finally comes to pass. For this effect to actually occur, the rumor or event needs to be:

- Widely known
- Growing in probability
- Noteworthy (potential for a major impact)
- Nearing the date it's expected to occur

The merger between the satellite radio companies XM and Sirius is a good example. There was unprecedented discussion in the media and among the investment community about the combination of the two companies. It was a noteworthy event since it would help both companies survive, and was expected to have major benefits such as millions in cost savings. The CEO of Sirius, Mel Karmazin, made frequent updates in press releases about the progress of the merger talks, and provided dates for when he expected that the regulatory bodies would rule on the matter.

The result was a widely followed rumor that excited investors. Traders held shares, or bought more, waiting for the good news of a

Trading Tactics: Buy the Rumor, Sell the Fact
(Continued)

merger to be announced. The expectation was that shares of both companies would spike upon any announcement.

Shares were trading as high as $2.75 the day before the merger announcement.

However, on July 25, 2008, when the merger was finally approved, the shares started falling.

Short-term traders had been anxiously waiting for the announcement so they could make a quick profit by selling into the news. Long-term investors looked to the merger as the beginning of a long, sustained uptrend in price. Both were surprised as the merger announcement actually set off a downward slide for the shares. The trading price of the merged company sank all the way down from its post-merger high of $2.75 to $0.11 within five months. (See Figure 1.4.)

What was the difference in Sirius at $2.75 and Sirius at $0.11 soon after? Nothing, besides the long-awaited and sought-after merger, which was supposed to take the satellite radio companies to the next level. Well, I don't think they expected the next level to be a share price that was 95 percent lower.

At the time of the merger announcement, there weren't any other major events in the near future that might help spike the prices.

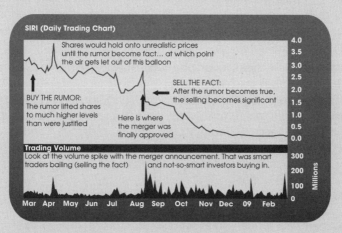

Figure 1.4   Sirius Satellite Radio Trading

(Continued)

Trading Tactics: Buy the Rumor, Sell the Fact
(*Continued*)

Speculators and long-term shareholders alike didn't have much to look forward to, now that the merger announcement had been made.

Overall, the stock suddenly didn't seem as exciting. The amount of optimistic speculation in the shares took a big hit, and investors were now forced to look at the company's fundamentals. The financials couldn't be ignored any longer.

The merger caused shares of Sirius and XM, which until now had been treated by investors as speculative plays, to be traded based on their operational results. In other words, the post-merger world didn't have any more speculative optimism. Instead, investors now started to look at the very ugly reality of the debt-ridden financials.

In fact, I wrote a lengthy article about the absolutely ridiculous balance sheets of the two companies on July 30, 2007. It was called "Sirius Trouble." Here are some excerpts, to give you an idea of the tone of my message:

> After extensively looking at the financials of both companies . . . they are both pretty brutal. So, what do you get when you combine two financially suspect companies? One bigger financially suspect company. . . .
>
> . . . via creative financings (such as issuing shares), they will heavily dilute the company. The surviving company steams on, but the value of the shares will be worth significantly less than they are now.

With satellite radio, everyone was buying the rumor. The smart money knew to sell the fact.

"Buy the rumor, sell the fact" plays out again and again on the markets. It's certainly not the exception, but rather the rule. Keeping this in mind will help you identify penny stocks that may trend upward, allowing you to ride the shares up for profits. Just make sure to escape your position before they come crashing back down to earth and to more realistic valuations.

In other words, buy the rumor, and sell the fact.

2

Getting Started in Penny Stocks

**Experience
Level I**
● ★★★★
You'll be surprised how easy it is to get started in penny stocks. In fact, you can even begin right now, this instant, with zero dollars.

I suggest you start by "paper trading." This simply means that you keep track of potential trades in stocks using imaginary money. This is actually one of the keys to my success. There is an entire section devoted to paper trading in chapter three.

You should paper trade until you feel comfortable with investing. This means understanding the way penny stocks "act," knowing the terminology, getting in touch with your own style, and getting a feel for the ins and outs of the market. Once you've accomplished all of that, you'll be a much more successful trader; only then should you start using real money. All you need to get started buying your first penny stock is:

- Money
- An online discount broker

Here's how it works:

- You deposit the money you want to invest into your online brokerage account.
- When you're interested in a stock, you buy it online through your brokerage account.

- The broker takes a very small commission (usually less than $10) for the trade.

You now hold the shares you purchased in the brokerage account, and can keep track of them and sell them online.

The Best Brokers

The online brokers are inexpensive. You can sign up and do everything else over the Internet, and will be up and running within days. Most brokers are straightforward, and they'll provide all the customer support you need to get set up.

Each broker has a different minimum amount required to open an account. Some will allow you to get set up with no money at all, while others ask you to deposit thousands up front.

Some brokers have a sliding commission scale, where you pay greater commissions if you have less money with them. For example, if you've got only $500 in your account, your commission rate is greater than for somebody who has $20,000.

If you are a *Peter Leeds Penny Stocks* subscriber, then you get to benefit from our extensive discount broker rankings. We have researched the brokers and ranked them based on "friendliness" toward trading low-priced stocks. We have already done the following:

- Called all of the brokers
- E-mailed them from PeterLeeds.com, explaining our project
- E-mailed them again, this time acting as potential clients
- Tracked their responses, looking for professionalism, helpfulness, and reply times

As well, we considered their:

- Policies
- Commission rates
- Hidden/special fees

Out of this research, we came up with our official list of the "Top Penny Stock–Friendly Brokers," which we make available to all subscribers of *Peter Leeds Penny Stocks.*

Experience Level 3

Trading Tactics: Dollar Cost Averaging

This can be a good strategy for newer investors, specifically when you are buying shares but are unsure of the best buy price. Instead of accumulating all at once, you buy in several smaller chunks over time.

For example, a small percentage of each of your paychecks could go toward buying the shares. Alternatively, you could buy once a month over the course of a year, or even over several years.

If you bought $1,000 worth each month, instead of putting in $12,000 up front, then you're *dollar cost averaging.* Sometimes you'll end up buying at a historically higher price, and sometimes you'll pay a historically lower price. The rest of the time (most of the time, in fact), the shares will be somewhere between these extremes.

Since you get your overall cost averaged, you don't need to try to buy at the very bottom, nor do you need to worry about acquiring the shares at the top. You shouldn't be concerned about the price you pay. Over time, your average cost will be somewhere in the middle of the high- and low-price extremes. You aren't going to get in at the lowest overall price, but you're also not going to pay the highest overall price.

In general, your average cost will be close to the average share price over the duration for which you dollar cost averaged. For example, over a year, with a new purchase every two weeks, your average cost will likely be close to the average share price in that 12-month period.

If you decide to dollar cost average, make sure to do so for a long enough time period to make it effective. For example, purchases over one year will give you a better average price than if you did it for three months. If you dollar cost averaged for only three months, you're not necessarily getting a meaningful benefit. You're paying an average for that short period, but that could be much higher or much lower than the prices you see for the rest of the year.

(Continued)

Trading Tactics: Dollar Cost Averaging (*Continued*)

Is it a good idea? Maybe. Perhaps for some it would be really effective. It's usually common among newer and less sophisticated investors because it's a safer way to buy and sell without needing to worry so much about the exact share price.

Dollar cost averaging may be a strategy to consider if you are unsure of:

- The current valuation
- What price to pay for the shares
- The price at which to sell shares
- Overall risk
- Future price direction

Dollar cost averaging can be a great trading strategy for newer or less confident investors. In some cases, it may even be appropriate for experienced traders. The decision on whether to incorporate such an approach will come down to your own skill level and motivations for trading.

What Penny Stock Should I Buy?

That's certainly the be-all, end-all question in this game. You will have more investment success by simply selecting the right penny stock in the first place than you will by doing everything else right.

What is the right penny stock? It's one that:

- Increases in price after you buy it
- Trades with enough volume that you can buy in and sell out easily
- Has a business that you understand

By looking for certain criteria, you can find just such a penny stock, and you can do it again and again. You simply need to learn *Leeds Analysis*, the standard in penny stock research, and then everything becomes easier.

Leeds Analysis is the most effective tool for finding the best penny stock opportunities, such as companies that:

- Have limited downside
- Enjoy massive upside potential
- Trade on legitimate exchanges
- Are fundamentally impressive
- Are beginning to see price momentum
- Benefit from a growing industry
- Have sector and economic trends going in their favor

When you find high-quality, fundamentally strong penny stocks with good management teams, patented technologies, and proven upside potential, you can really multiply your money.

How the Market Works

You don't buy shares from the stock market. You actually buy them from (or sell them to) other investors. The stock market is simply the middle ground, a place for investors' orders to meet up.

Think of it like eBay. You don't actually buy an item from eBay, you buy it from the seller, but you need eBay to act as the go-between. The stock market is exactly such a go-between for investors.

Just like on eBay, if you're trying to buy, then you're a bidder. On the market, the price you are willing to pay for shares is your "bid" price.

Current shareholders looking to sell shares know how much money they want for the stock. That price is their "ask" price, which is the amount they are "asking" to receive that would make them willing to let their shares go.

When a bid price is high enough and an ask price is low enough for the two to meet up, then a trade takes place. Assume you want to buy ABC Inc. If you bid $1.00 a share, but the lowest ask price is \$1.50, then you won't get the shares, and the seller won't get rid of them. However, if the seller dropped his ask to \$1.35 and you raised your bid to \$1.35, you would wind up buying the shares. In this example, you would have paid \$1.35 per share for ABC Inc.

There are many sources to explain the basics of trading, such as *Understanding Penny Stocks*, and it is not my intention to go into elaborate detail here. For brand-new investors, I'll quickly touch on one more important concept, the two types of trade orders, before we get into the really powerful stuff. If you're already an experienced stock market investor, by all means skip the next section.

 ## Market versus Limit Orders

To buy or sell shares, there are two types of trading orders:

1. Market orders
2. Limit orders

Market order: You trade the stock at the currently best available price.

With a *market order* to buy, you pay whatever the current market (ask) price is. With large orders in thinly traded penny stocks, this can result in your purchase pushing the price up while you are buying, and potentially costing you more per share than you had expected.

Imagine you entered a market order to buy 1,000 shares of ABC stock. You'll get the 1,000 shares, but if the lowest ask (the price sellers are willing to accept) at that time is \$1.40, then you end up paying \$1.40 per share. If the lowest ask had been \$1.95, then you'd pay \$1.95. That's quite a difference in price!

You can probably see why using a market order can result in potentially paying more than you had expected—you had no control over the price you ended up having to pay. With penny stocks, paying more than you wanted to is common when you use market orders, so traders need to protect themselves. Thankfully, there is a way to do so, and it's called a *limit order.*

Limit order: You specify the price you are willing to pay.

You decide what price you will pay for the shares, and the trade will take place only if you get the shares at that price, or an even more advantageous one. You can also use limit orders when you are selling, giving up the shares only if you get the price you choose, or an even higher one.

With a limit order you can decide that you will not pay more than X per share. You won't overpay, but you are also not guaranteed to get any or all of the shares you wanted. Imagine that you decided to buy ABC stock, but didn't want to pay more than $1.25 per share. Using a limit order at $1.25 protects your maximum cost. If the only shares for sale are asking $1.40, your trade won't take place at all, but at least you didn't pay more than you had wanted.

I don't give trading advice, and you must decide what's best for you, but I will give you my strong and educated opinion. It is always best with penny stocks to use limit orders rather than market orders, and this applies for both buying and selling.

If you buy with a market order, you might end up paying more than you had wanted to. When it comes to penny stocks, beginning traders should only and always use limit orders.

Once in a while, it may be appropriate for more experienced traders to use a market order. For example, sometimes when I'm aggressively accumulating a position, I use market orders to snatch up big blocks of shares. However, I do not suggest this approach to anyone except highly experienced traders.

Trading Tactics: Half Down

If you've ever been on the losing side of a stock trade, especially if you held on hoping those shares would go back to where you bought them, then you've been introduced to what I call the "Half Down" principle.

Quick question: If your shares drop half in value, how much do they have to go back up to reach breakeven?

Guess what, it's not 50 percent. It's 100 percent.

Picture a stock that falls from $2.00 to $1.00. It has fallen 50 percent in value. Now it's at $1.00, so how much does it need to rise to return to $2.00? It needs to increase in value by $1.00, so it would require an increase of 100 percent from the current price.

This unfortunate law of mathematics really puts investing into perspective. Even a 20 percent drop will need a 25 percent increase to get back to the start. A 90 percent drop needs a 900 percent gain to get back to where it began. Perhaps this is why investing can sometimes feel like you're swimming upstream—any losses you take will need to be overshadowed by any subsequent gains.

This is the unfortunate and unavoidable truth of the Half Down principle. Make sure to cut your losses early, as discussed in the Limiting Losses Trading Tactic in Chapter 5. Use Leeds Analysis to buy into high-quality companies with great upside potential that are less likely to introduce you to the dreaded Half Down concept.

 The Best Markets

The most effective and safest markets for penny stock trading are:

- Nasdaq
- OTC-BB (Over the Counter Bulletin Board, a subsidiary of Nasdaq)
- Amex

These markets have strict regulations and reporting requirements, ensuring that the companies are more transparent and
accountable.

We avoid the pink-sheet markets because, in general, the
pink-sheet stocks trade with very low volume, very weak reporting
requirements, and very few regulations. It is more difficult to find a
very good investment, and even if it goes up in price you may sometimes have trouble selling the shares.

We have also been looking at Canadian markets:

- Toronto Stock Exchange
- Toronto Venture Exchange

Both of these Canadian markets have thousands of penny stocks,
and the regulations and reporting requirements are just as good as
those found with the OTC-BB and other higher-end U.S. markets.

CHAPTER 3

Avoid Your Rough Start

MY ROCKY START

I learned about penny stocks the hard way.

By 14 years old I had saved up $3,600, which is a lot of money, especially for a kid. I wasn't given the money, but rather worked hard and saved it up, month after month, for a few years. At the same time that my friends were buying comic books and accessories for their BMX bikes, I was quietly building up a small fortune (as far as a 14-year-old kid is concerned).

I worked a bunch of jobs that took zero skill, and that no one could possibly enjoy doing: pulling weeds, moving rocks, clearing out junk. They didn't pay well, but I also didn't have any expenses.

They say that jobs like that are supposed to build character. I don't know about that, but I do remember really hating the work, and I don't think I became a better person by doing it. I figured that there has to be a better way to make money.

I ran a few miniature enterprises—selling 75-cent chocolate bars to my three older sisters for $1.50 apiece, or lending them money at a low, family discount interest rate of only 1 percent per day. One of my most successful ventures was getting a brick of 80 cherry bomb firecrackers, opening it up, and selling each one for 25 cents. Sold individually, the value of that brick of cherry bombs represented a markup of five times!

At this point I was ambitious and confident and sitting on $3,600, which to a 14-year-old kid was all the money in the world. I wondered how I could turn this money into even more, preferably without having to work.

Then I had the answer: *the stock market!*

So, what stocks could I buy for $3,600? I could get 20 or 50 shares of some major blue-chip company, which may or may not go anywhere at all. Was I really going to sit on a dozen shares of IBM or GE, then maybe in five years take my 15 percent profit? I would love to say that I have that kind of patience, but I absolutely do not. I would love to say that I'd be happy with small and steady returns, but I absolutely wouldn't.

My next thought was to get involved in the tiny companies, these so-called "penny stocks," because those would be the ones that move fastest, are the most exciting, and have the potential for big time returns. So I made up my mind. I would buy a penny stock.

Now see if you can count how many mistakes I made. I looked through the newspaper (back in the pre-Internet days when you got your stock quotes from the business section), and looked for one of the lowest-priced shares.

There it was: Siberian Pacific Resources, trading at $0.14. The ticker symbol "SIB" jumped out at me like it was the only stock on the page. My mind was made up, the decision was done. I was going to buy shares of SIB. Siberian Pacific Resources, here I come.

Of course, I didn't know anything at all about the company, but what could go wrong? I mean, if it's on the stock market, it must be a well-run company, right?

I wasn't a complete and total idiot, although this story seems to say the opposite about me. I knew that the price could go down after I bought it, and I reasoned with myself that if the shares start dropping, then I'll learn my lesson, cash out, and take my loss. In fact, if it even dropped toward 11 or 12 cents, I would bail.

I wasn't old enough to have my own trading account, so I bought the shares through my mother's broker. At various prices, I scooped up 30,000 shares of Siberian with my $3,600. Then I did what many newer investors do—I checked the stock price. I checked it again five minutes later, then again every chance I could. I obsessed about the shares, continually doing math in my head. I would make $300 for every penny the shares increased! I was so excited!

After the first week Siberian had dropped from 14 to 13 cents. My loss was $300 so far. I got a little nervous. Of course, I knew it could go back up, so I wasn't too distraught. I also figured that if it dropped any more, then I would take my lumps and sell my shares, lesson learned.

Then it happened. The stock got "halted." *Halted?* I didn't know what that meant. I had never heard the term before. I didn't understand.

I called the stock exchange. They said, "The company isn't going to be in business any more, they don't want to continue with the listing requirements of the exchange, and they don't really have any operations. They voluntarily halted themselves, meaning they won't trade anymore."

I said, "Can I get my money back?"

They said, "Sure, if you can find someone to buy your shares." They knew, as I knew, even as they said it, that *no one* was going to buy these shares. I'm also not the type to correct my mistake by dumping it off onto someone else.

I did call the Siberian Resources headquarters. It turns out that they were based in England, which I didn't know until that moment. It sounded like the woman must have been answering the phone in her basement. Now don't get me wrong, it wasn't a scam or anything like that—Siberian did turn out to have been a legitimate company that at one time did have some major operations. Unfortunately for me, that was a couple of years before I jumped on board.

I asked the woman, "Can I sell my shares?" She sounded a lot like the man at the stock exchange I had spoken with, when she said, "If you can find somebody to buy them." In that moment, with that reply, all the money I had worked so hard to build up absolutely vaporized in my mind. It had already vaporized in reality weeks earlier, the moment I invested in SIB.

Siberian Pacific Resources had become just an afterthought in the minds of its management team, all of whom had apparently moved on to new or better opportunities.

So in two weeks I had lost all of my money.

I learned really quickly that when you lose money, you lose a lot more than just the dollars. You lose confidence. You lose ambition, and pride, and hope. At the same time, you gain a lot of bad things: embarrassment, regret, and anxiety.

Oddly, it turned out to be one of the best things that could have happened. If I could lose that much money that quickly, then there must be a way on the stock market to *make* that much money that quickly. I set about trying to find that way. As far as I was concerned, the market had taken $3,600 from me, and I wanted to get it back. Little did I know that I would make that much money back, and I would do it hundreds of times over.

First, fresh off my harsh lesson, I dumped my cocky attitude. I also took full responsibility for my mistake. It was not the fault of the management of Siberian Pacific Resources, it was not the fault of the stock exchange, it was not my broker's fault. It was mine, and mine alone, and I took ownership of that.

I took the financial world seriously now. It can be like a game, but it is not a game. It is serious, with major upside and downside, and your actions have tangible real-world results.

I started with a blank mind, admitted I knew nothing about stocks, and set about learning as much as I could. My biggest key to success was in doing extensive paper-trading. I also focused not just on how to pick stocks that go up, but also on how to avoid the pitfalls.

I read all the major stock market books from all the major stock market masters, like Peter Lynch, Warren Buffett, and a few dozen people whose names you won't recognize. I basically became a sponge for technical analysis, fundamental analysis, dozens of different trading strategies, and basically everything I could get my hands on. I consumed dozens and dozens of financial books. I took pieces from each of their strategies.

I continued to refine my approach as I continually learned more new ideas. Through trial and error, testing, learning, and paper-trading successes and failures, I noticed that I started becoming pretty good at investing. More accurately, the method I developed, which I called Leeds Analysis, started becoming pretty good at investing.

The Birth of Leeds Analysis

With all types of investments, but especially with penny stocks, investors need to take all factors into account. This is the major driving principle behind Leeds Analysis, the successful trading methodology that I've developed.

Out of significant paper-trading, ongoing research, and in-the-trenches experiences, I developed and continually refined Leeds Analysis. It was always specifically targeted toward penny stocks, those shares trading at under $5. It took into account the fact that these shares often trade on lighter volume and generally experience more significant volatility than most other stocks.

I always compare buying a penny stock to buying a used car. There's nothing wrong with buying a *used car* (although there is a bad connotation associated with the term). In fact, you can get a really good value in a used car if you know what to look for. If you don't know what to look for, you're more likely to get burned.

Picture a used car that looks amazing—it's the model and year you want and the color you want, it has great fuel economy, and it looks good inside and under the hood. Most people would take it for a drive, and if it didn't make any strange noises from the engine they'd go back and haggle for a good purchase price.

Now, what you might not have seen is that the air conditioner runs for only three minutes before it conks out, the driveshaft is about to fall off the car completely, it's been in two accidents, and one of the pistons is going to snap sometime in the next few months. If there were such a thing as Leeds Analysis for cars, all of these issues would have been considered.

Much like penny stocks, any one negative factor (like those I mentioned in the used car example) could derail the entire value of your purchase. It is the same for tiny companies such as those Leeds Analysis will help you discover, where any single issue could cause the shares to plummet: one lawsuit, one major customer canceling its account, one product recall, the death of the CEO.

A major blue-chip corporation can survive one or two or even a dozen issues, but a small, $10 million penny stock company with six employees doesn't have that luxury.

The bigger something is, the more energy it takes to move it. The smaller something is, the less energy it takes to move it. The laws of physics, it would seem, apply to penny stocks as well.

Experience
Level 3

Trading Tactics: Gapping

Sometimes a stock starts trading at a different price than where it closed the day before, which is called *gapping*. Newer investors tend to get confused by this concept, and my team often fields questions about it.

Picture a stock that closed the previous day at $1.25. Before today's markets open, that stock would probably be set to trade somewhere around that price point.

However, it's possible that it starts the day being bought and sold at a significantly different level, whether it's far higher or far lower than the previous day's $1.25 close. For example, it could start trading at $1.70, or perhaps $0.55.

Maybe this stock doesn't even trade at first, but when you get a quote you see that the shares are bid only $0.40 and the ask is a mere $0.55, far lower than the previous day's $1.25 close.

Trading Tactics: Gapping (*Continued*)

People get confused when they see this: *Why is a $1.25 stock being bid at only $0.40? Shouldn't it be $1.25?*

It might even make its first trade at these low levels. *Three thousand shares at 50 cents? I thought it was a $1.25 stock!* That's the way a free and efficient stock market works. In our example here, there may have been news out overnight, or just a dry-up in investor interest. Gapping up and gapping down are just symptoms of such market forces.

Less experienced traders often get confused, because they think that the last price at which a stock traded is what those shares are "worth." If shares are trading at $2.40, they believe anyone can buy a share for $2.40, or sell a share for $2.40, and that the stock is actually worth $2.40. Not true.

They also think that, since the shares closed the day before at $2.40, as in our example, they must start trading the next day at $2.40. Also not true.

Shares are like diamonds, cars, houses, and baseball cards. They are worth whatever you can get someone to pay for them. Whatever that value is, it changes instantly and often, depending on such factors as:

- Supply
- Demand
- Motivation for the purchase
- Motivation for the sale
- Prices of comparable investments
- Historical long-term and short-term trend in prices

Gapping is usually, but not always, brought on by news or events when the markets are closed. A gold mine might gap up from one day's close price to the next day's open if the price of gold spiked dramatically higher overnight.

ABC Inc. might be trading at $2.05 one day and open with its first trade at $1.75 the next. This could be a result of some major news when the market was closed, or perhaps it's just symptomatic of being a thinly traded stock.

Just keep in mind that any stock can open at any price on any day. That is the entire point of a free-flowing capitalist stock market. People decide what something is worth, and that worth doesn't have to be based on the final closing price of the previous day.

An Overview of Leeds Analysis

To look into every aspect of a company, and to do this with dozens or hundreds of companies, or even thousands, as is the case at *Peter Leeds Penny Stocks*, might seem like an impossible task. In many ways it would be, if not for one major truth. Companies are actually similar in many ways from one to the next. This applies even when they're different sizes, in different industries, and have different business models. Usually two seemingly opposite companies will have more in common than they have in differences.

Due to the similarities of all corporations, we are able to apply Leeds Analysis to many companies, guiding ourselves with a basic understanding of positive factors and potential warning signs. This applies to every aspect of any operational corporation.

Consider that every company has a way that it:

- Makes money
- Spends money
- Saves money
- Deals with debt and liabilities
- Produces products/provides services
- Attracts new clients
- Deals with current clients
- Hires employees
- Protects its intellectual properties, and so on

Also consider that every company may be:

- In an industry that is growing or shrinking
- Working on new products/services or terminating old ones
- In a sector considered "hot" or "cold"
- Diluting its shares, or buying back more, and so on

Over the years, if we missed a factor in our analysis that turned out to be material to the share price performance, we upgraded Leeds Analysis to reflect that consideration from that moment onward. It has evolved to such a degree that it's rare to get surprised by a stock that you have put through Leeds Analysis (although it does sometimes happen). In fact, the current version of Leeds Analysis as described in this book should be considered *LA version 7.0.4.*

Leeds Analysis considers every aspect of a company. Our system is very demanding, and we not only look to avoid warning signs, we also look for what we have found to be the indicators that point to strong upside potential for the shares. We avoid the duds and migrate toward those companies that are poised to appreciate in price. That's why 95 percent of companies do not pass the test and only 5 percent make the cut. That's also why Leeds Analysis has rapidly become the standard in penny stock research, and it boasts such compelling results.

Due Diligence

I'm going to tell you something you've heard many times before: "You need to do your due diligence."

What does that really mean? In most cases, it's used as a disclaimer, tacked onto every financial advertisement and web site and newsletter. You've probably heard that phrase so often that your mind automatically shuts it out.

However, the message is actually very important. It simply means "Know what you are getting into and take responsibility." If you perform due diligence properly, you will know the company, the business it's engaged in, why you're investing, and what you expect to get out of it.

Even if you're getting your penny stock picks from the Peter Leeds service, you still must perform your own due diligence. Don't take a stock pick from any source without first assessing the company yourself, and judging whether the investment's situation makes sense for your strategy.

Due diligence simply involves looking into the investment your-self until you:

- Have a good idea of what you're investing in.
- Understand the reasons why you're getting involved with it.
- Know what you expect the company and the share price to do next.
- Are ready to take responsibility for your own trade decisions and results.

Despite being extremely important, *due diligence* is one of the most misunderstood terms in the financial world. Most people feel like they are doing due diligence because they check out a compa-ny's web site, or review the latest balance sheet, or read some press releases.

The sad fact is that most people actually have their mind made up before they do any significant research, and they sim-ply use the process of "looking into the company" just to rein-force their trading decision. Think of it like watching a political speech—if you are a Democrat, a democratic speaker might sound great to you, but a republican speaker may rub you the wrong way. Now, if you're a Republican watching the exact same speech, then that would hold true in reverse. You are seeing things through colored lenses.

When it comes to stock market due diligence, try to be like an undecided voter. Keep your head clear, and treat your mind as a blank slate. Importantly, don't get excited and fall in love with the company you're researching.

Done well, due diligence will involve:

- Common sense
- Research time
- Proven research and analysis techniques, like Leeds Analysis

Leeds Analysis, while thorough and effective, is not a substitute for your own due diligence. It will, however, really streamline and improve your technique and potentially improve your stock market returns significantly.

With due diligence, remember that you are doing a lot more than judging whether the penny stock is a good investment. You are also judging whether it represents a better investment opportunity than all the other penny stocks out there. If the shares end up making a respectable 25 percent, you still have the lost opportunity of potentially putting your money into something that made even more.

Once you've done your due diligence on your investment prospects, both in your own style and by performing Leeds Analysis, you are ready for possibly the most active and exciting part of trading penny stocks: buying them!

After the majority of your due diligence is done, and you are preparing to make a purchase, the best way to proceed is to:

- Look into many companies that passed your due diligence.
- Make sure they meet your investment strategies and goals.
- Watch these companies over time, and continually get to know them better.
- Pare down your list of penny stocks as you gain more clarity.
- Watch for buying opportunities and price dips (see Chapter Eight, "Technical Analysis").
- Get involved in a few of your best opportunities. (Make sure to keep diversified.)
- Scale in (see Chapter Six, "Trading Tactics: Scaling In and Scaling Out").

Stock Trades without Due Diligence

Among those who actually perform their due diligence, which is the minority, it is usually only surface research and it's very subjective.

Rather than looking into a company deeply enough, you'll see people making trading decisions based on tips from friends or some comment in the news or on a web site.

If someone comes to you with a stock pick and claims that you should get involved, try exposing this person's ignorance by asking a few questions. For example:

- Who is the CEO? (Most won't even know the answer!)
- How long has the CEO been with the company?
- Where did the CEO work prior to this company?
- How many shares does key management own?
- How do the holdings of management compare to three years prior?
- What are the revenue levels?
- Who is the company's largest competitor?
- What is its market share and how does that compare to three years ago?

The vast majority of people won't know any of the answers to these questions. If they haven't done proper due diligence, why should you trust the information? A lot of people make bad investment decisions because someone else comes to them excited about a stock and with a good story. Don't be one of these victims.

On the other hand, if you meet someone who knows the answers to these questions, she may have done a lot of her own due diligence and so her stock may be worth a look after all. You then need to do your own research on top of hers, and make sure that this company matches your investment style and tactics.

The biggest danger to investors is free stock picks. This applies to spam faxes, mailings, and phone calls, but it is most prevalent on the Internet. Every free stock pick has hidden motivations and misleading information. Ask yourself, "Why am I getting this free stock pick? What's in it for the source?" They have an angle, and it almost certainly involves making money while you lose money.

If someone tells you about a stock, or you hear about it online or in the news, and you decide to check it out, then start from scratch. Forget anything he told you about the company, other than the name and ticker symbol. Sit down with an open mind and learn everything you need to know to make an informed decision that you'll feel comfortable with. Don't be afraid to walk away if you find any warning signs at all.

Most stock promoters are getting paid by the company to drive the share price up, or they hold hundreds of thousands (or millions) of shares and want to cash out for a profit while you buy in based on their misleading information. They gloss over the company's downside in their comments, and put the company's best foot forward so that you'll buy the stock. They're making a lot of money by misleading you. They are hoping to take money out of your pocket by putting some lipstick on a pig and promoting it to you.

Any free web site that claims they do not get paid by or compensated by the companies they talk about certainly owns shares in the stocks they promote. If they say they don't own shares, then look for their contact phone number. They are up to something, and in the stock market world, if they don't have a phone number you shouldn't trust their web site. This applies to both free and paid subscription web sites.

Generally, legitimate services will provide a phone number. Call it to make sure it's not a fake, because a few web sites have posted fictitious contact information. If they do answer, just say you were calling to make sure it was a real phone number and that you wanted to know that the service is legitimate. They will understand why you are asking.

Dishonest people give the industry a bad name, and it has effects even on legitimate, professional services like *Peter Leeds Penny Stocks*. That's why I came up with the industry's first *100 Percent Unbiased Guarantee*.

Trading Tactics: Microsoft Was Never a Penny Stock

Microsoft was *never* a penny stock. You've almost certainly heard otherwise, but it's one of the most common investment "misunderstandings." Microsoft went public in 1986 at $21, started increasing in price, and never looked back.

Table 3.1 summarizes Microsoft's nine common stock splits since the initial public offering on March 13, 1986.

I've even heard people socializing at events, whispering that phrase like a juicy rumor: "You know, Microsoft used to be a penny stock. We should look into this ABC corporation, because they're gonna be the next Microsoft!"

Here's where the confusion comes in. Looking at a long-term trading chart of Microsoft, which includes data going back to its IPO on March 13, 1986, it looks like the stock started trading at a couple of cents, then got to much higher levels where it trades today. (See Figure 3.1.) What most people don't realize is that that's just the chart adjusting the original prices for the impact of numerous stock splits.

Here's what I mean: If Microsoft is trading today at $30, that's what the long-term chart will show. However, if the stock split 2 for 1 (2 new shares for each 1 old share), it might then be trading near $15. The chart will reflect the $15 price. However, all prices on that chart previous

Table 3.1   Microsoft's Common Stock Splits

Split Date	Split Factor	Closing Price $ Before/After	1 Original Share Becomes:
September 18, 87	2 for 1	114.50/53.50	2
April 12, 90	2 for 1	120.75/60.75	4
June 26, 91	3 for 2	100.75/68.00	6
June 12, 92	3 for 2	112.50/75.75	9
May 20, 94	2 for 1	97.75/50.63	18
December 6, 96	2 for 1	152.87/81.75	36
February 20, 98	2 for 1	155.13/81.63	70
March 26, 99	2 for 1	178.13/92.38	144
February 14, 03	2 for 1	48.30/24.96	288

Trading Tactics: Microsoft Was Never a Penny Stock
(*Continued*)

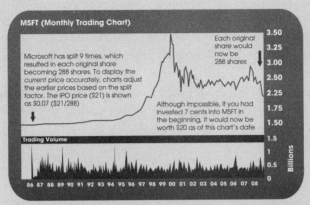

MSFT (Monthly Trading Chart)

Microsoft has split 9 times, which resulted in each original share becoming 288 shares. To display the current price accurately, charts adjust the earlier prices based on the split factor. The IPO price ($21) is shown as $0.07 ($21/288)

Each original share would now be 288 shares

Although impossible, if you had invested 7 cents into MSFT in the beginning, it would now be worth $20 as of this chart's date

Trading Volume

86 87 88 89 90 91 92 93 94 95 96 97 98 99 00 01 02 03 04 05 06 07 08

Figure 3.1   Microsoft's Long-Term Trading

to the split will be cut in half. If it looked like Microsoft had started trading at 4 cents on its IPO date, now that chart will show that it started trading at 2 cents.

Each of Microsoft's share splits over the years (and there were many of them) further compress the historical data down, simply so that the chart can accurately show today's current share price.

Picture a stock that started trading at $10 per share. A year later it has a 10-for-1 stock split. A trading chart will then show that stock had originally started trading at $1 to adjust for the split factor.

Next time you hear someone talking about how Microsoft used to be a penny stock, you can debunk that. It's a rampant investment rumor, but now you know the truth.

The 100 Percent Unbiased Guarantee

Peter Leeds Penny Stocks guarantees its research is completely impartial.

No kickbacks! Peter Leeds employees and directors never receive any compensation whatsoever from any company we cover.

No pump-and-dump! Some newsletters buy stock in a company and then hype it to subscribers. As the stock price peaks, the service stops talking up the shares and dumps them all at a fat profit. After the "pump-and-dump," the stock price collapses and subscribers are left holding the bag. We never buy or sell any *Peter Leeds Penny Stock* picks, or in any way benefit from trading in their shares.

No personal stakes! All employees and directors are prohibited from taking a trading position or having any form of vested interest in any Peter Leeds stock pick.

No scalping! Scalping is recommending a stock to investors while selling it at the same time. We never engage in this unethical practice.

No incentives! We never have any self-serving reason for choosing one penny stock instead of another. Our only goal is to uncover the penny stock winners that will provide the greatest benefit to our subscribers.

No tips to friends and family! The strict rules behind our guarantee of 100 percent unbiased research also apply to our friends and family members. We never mention our picks to friends, family members, or anyone, until we alert our subscribers. Most other services have loose lips that put your interests dead last.

Why Peter Leeds Is the Leader

The vast majority of financial newsletters are not very professional, not very accurate, and not very trustworthy. That is why they don't provide working phone numbers, never get any media coverage, and have little more than a homemade web site. You'll see that the average newsletter is a one-man show, probably operated from someone's bedroom when he is not at his real job. With these one-man shows you should have concerns about the quality of information and professionalism of their operations and be afraid of their hidden motivations.

Trading Tactics: Reverse Split

All investors, but especially penny stock investors, dread the *reverse split*. This is when a company consolidates its shares, so that for every five shares (for example) you end up with one.

The theory is that your one share should be worth five times as much, so while you have fewer shares the value of your holdings has remained unchanged. This is *not* how it plays out in reality, however, since most reverses are symptomatic of a company that is struggling.

Companies that enact reverse splits are usually having trouble keeping their share price up. In most cases, the underlying companies are simply trying to meet the listing requirements of the exchange upon which they trade.

To trade on the Nasdaq, for example, the share price must be at least $1.00. If a company's stock price drops to $0.25, it's in danger of being booted off the exchange altogether.

A quick fix for the company: Just enact a 4-for-1 reverse split. The result would see the company with one-fourth as many outstanding shares, but those shares should theoretically trade for about $1 each (4 shares at $0.25 each become 1 share worth $1.00).

In actual practice, the company from our example would be more likely to enact a 10-for-1 or even 20-for-1 reverse, taking the shares up toward $2.50 or $5.00, giving the company some breathing room above the $1.00 threshold requirement.

Generally, a reverse split sees the shares fall in price in two stages: before the split once it's first announced; then even more after the split gets enacted. A reverse split is generally a sign of a struggling company, or one that is on the way down, at least in recent months.

Thus, a company might reverse split 10 shares into 1, but usually the end result is that the value of the 1 new share ends up being worth less than the original 10. Be wary of reverse splits and of companies that may enact such a move.

A truly healthy company that's growing strongly is more likely to enact the opposite of the reverse split, which is simply a regular share split. A 2-for-1 split sees each share of the stock become two shares, with each being theoretically worth half as much. For example, a $30

(Continued)

Trading Tactics: Reverse Split (*Continued*)

stock splits 2 for 1, converting every individual share into 2, worth $15 each.

In general, a company enacting a 2-for-1, or 3-for-1, or even 5-for-1 split will benefit in overall share price. The value of each share will be less, but shareholders will have 2, or 3, or 5 times as many shares. Those shares then often increase in price, as the share split is welcomed by investors and is generally the sign of a healthy, growing company.

Here are some of the ways *Peter Leeds Penny Stocks* is superior:

- Phone support at 1-866-MY-LEEDS
- Full e-mail support
- Team of staff, not just a one-man show
- Extensive media coverage
- Largest subscriber base
- Leading results
- By far the greatest depth of information
- Daily updates
- Quarterly Quick Fix reports (10 Stocks Undervalued, Undiscovered, Under $1)
- More than 50 bonus Profit Maker articles

The ways *Peter Leeds Penny Stocks* is superior don't end there. We encourage you to see for yourself, if you're not already a subscriber, by visiting us at www.PeterLeeds.com. Take a free no-risk, no-cost trial. Join the thousands who keep benefiting from Peter Leeds, the Penny Stock Professional.

 Paper Trading

I cannot stress it enough: Paper trading is the key to learning the ropes of penny stock trading and the fastest way to develop a tremendously effective strategy.

Simply put, it means that you keep track of imaginary trades in real penny stocks with imaginary money. For example, you pretend you have $100,000 to invest, and you keep track of which stocks you "would have" bought.

If you aren't already an experienced investor, you should definitely get started by paper trading. In fact, extensive paper trading early in my career was one of the keys to my success. It has many advantages:

- Zero financial risk.
- Zero costs.
- Practice with more money than you actually have.
- Make more trades than you would have.
- Very fast learning curve.
- Watch your results in real time on the live market.

After your paper-trading exercise has gone on for many months, you can look back and see how you fared, where you made the most money, which strategies worked, and which strategies did not.

Here are some good reasons for paper trading:

- To learn the ropes of investing, including choosing and monitoring stocks and deciding on your entry and exit prices
- To develop an investment strategy or methodology
- To test or refine an existing investment strategy or information source
- To keep an eye on stocks that interest you, with the purpose of uncovering accumulation or sale opportunities
- For fun
- To decide on the best sources of information, quotes, charts, news, and tracking

There are any number of ways that you can start up and monitor your own paper-trading strategy. What I describe here are simply the approaches that have had the best results in the past and have garnered the most positive feedback.

However, before you decide on an approach you first need to decide on your goals for this exercise:

- Are you trying to uncover stocks to invest in?
- Are you testing a new investment methodology and want to see what results you can attain with it?
- Do you just want to learn how to trade penny stocks?

Your answers to these questions may influence your paper-trading strategy.

There are seven parameters that can be customized to your own personal preferences:

1. Starting cash
2. Timeframe
3. Screening (criteria for stocks)
4. Pricing (recording of transaction prices)
5. Trading activity parameters/rules
6. Stock monitoring methods
7. Paper trading tracking methods

Starting Cash

Generally begin with enough cash to let you get a feel for the market, and experiment with several different stocks.

If you have $1,000 real money to eventually invest, and you know that you will be putting that into two different penny stocks, you'll certainly need to be highly selective in your choice of stocks. Therefore, you will also want to encourage a paper-trading strategy that forces you to be highly selective while you're learning the ropes so that the jump to real trading will be relatively parallel.

However, if you keep the imaginary cash level too low, you may not get involved with very many paper-trading decisions. Thus, you may not learn very much from the exercise. A paper-trading exercise with $1,000 is almost pointless, because the learning curve will be quite low and there won't be a lot of decisions to make from day to day.

I feel that traders should start with between 5 and 10 times their real money level for paper trading. If you eventually will be using $3,000 to invest, an imaginary starting level of $20,000 or $30,000 cash would be appropriate to trade many different stocks without becoming too unrealistic.

I also believe that for paper trading, especially for penny stocks, you should have a minimum of $10,000 imaginary starting cash.

Keep the amount a nice, round number so that it's easy to tell if you are up or down, and by how much.

Timeframe

Decide when the paper-trading exercise will begin and end. This enables you to see how much money you could've made or lost within a set time period.

Note that paper trading exercises do not have to end at all. Instead, you can see how your penny stocks have fared month by month, year by year, indefinitely.

I suggest that you paper trade for many months before getting involved in the markets with actual cash. At the same time I understand that you will be very anxious and excited to begin making these trades with real money, especially if your strategies are paying off. Be patient and give your paper trading techniques time to prove that they are effective before you make the jump to real money.

Screening

You may want to limit the theater of paper trading by looking only at certain stocks on certain markets, or buying only into shares that are below a certain price point. Alternatively, you may decide to have the pool of potential stocks literally unlimited just as it is in real life.

I suggest that you do not use pink-sheet issues for paper trading, because in real life you may not be able to sell those shares when you want. Just because the quote is $1.55 doesn't mean that you would be able to exit your position at that price, or at all, since it's on the unreliable pink-sheet market, which may create misleading results in your paper trading.

Screening can be done by choosing:

- The price of the stocks you will be paper trading
- The market(s) that you will focus on
- Specific industries or sectors (e.g., no biotech, mostly technology, etc.)

It is based mainly on your own preferences and should be in line with the types of penny stocks you will eventually be trading. Of course, I also understand that you may not know what types of stocks interest you yet. Hopefully, paper trading will give you a feel for many different industries, markets, and prices of stocks.

Trading Prices

Decide on your method of recording share prices for your trades. During any given trading day shares open at a certain level, move around between an upper and lower price for the day, and then close somewhere within that range. This makes it difficult to know exactly what you would have paid for your shares.

If you are trading for real, you can know the price you paid for shares because it will be part of your trade receipt. You will be able to access it through your online broker, and you may have even used a limit order to set the price of the trade.

With paper trading you will not have that luxury. You need to choose how you will record the prices of the stocks you buy and sell. For example, you may decide that you will use the day's closing price for each stock, whether you are buying or selling. You decide to buy 5,000 shares of TMED on Tuesday, so you take Tuesday's closing price for TMED to calculate how much the 5,000 shares cost you.

While the above example is the easiest for tracking purposes, it is the most unrealistic. This is because you can't tell your broker, "I'd like to buy at the closing price for the day." Instead, any trade you make will come during the day, and the transaction will happen at the price the shares are trading the moment you send in your order.

Thus, if you have the time to check stock prices throughout the day, you may want to get a quote for the price of the shares at the moment you make your buy or sell decision. If the market is closed, then look to when they open again the next day and try your imaginary order again then.

If you prefer to approach it differently, there are other markers you could use. For example, there's the intraday high or low, the day's average price, or the opening price. These all sacrifice some realism for the sake of simplicity and may cause aberrations when you apply your strategy to real-money situations.

If you are thinking about using limit orders, which you should be, make a note of your buy or sell limit price upon deciding to make a trade. Then, at the end of the day, see if the shares hit your target price.

For example, you decide to buy 5,000 ABC at $1.15 or lower. You later check and see that the shares hit $1.10 at one point, so if your order had been in you would have gotten the shares. You record the purchase of 5,000 shares at $1.15.

On the other hand, if the shares had never hit your limit price (say the lowest price on the day was $1.20), mark it up as an attempted (but not filled) purchase, and look to the following trading day to try again.

Trading Activity

Decide whether you will allow trading in and out of stocks. Some paper traders keep things simple by having a "buy-and-hold" mentality. I do not see any reason you should not be able to sell your shares, take the cash, and reinvest. Just be sure to keep extensive notes, come up with realistic prices, and charge a realistic broker commission for every trade.

Monitoring

Decide ahead of time how you will monitor the stocks you are following. Try to use the same sources throughout the exercise, and they should also be the sources you'll be using once you begin trading with real money.

If your purpose for paper trading is partially to decide on which information sources are best, then try them all. Just keep track of which you were using so you'll be able to look back later and decide which proved most useful, and more importantly, most accurate.

Tracking

To fully benefit, you'll need to keep extensive notes on your paper-trading exercise. Keep everything recorded so you can look back to uncover which trading strategies worked best.

Make notes on the following nine criteria and instances:

1. Starting cash.
2. Starting timeframe.
3. Ending timeframe, if any.
4. Any screens, which are meant to limit the types of stocks you can trade.
5. Starting value of all the major markets, including Nasdaq, NYSE, and AMEX.
6. Specific reasons why you chose each stock.
7. All buy and sell orders that get filled, including the stock you bought, the volume, the price per share, the total cost, and your imaginary broker fees.
8. All buy and sell orders that do not get filled, including the stock you attempted to buy, your limit price, and the volume of shares.
9. Keep track of the value of stocks and remaining cash at scheduled intervals (for example, every month on the first day).

By completing point 1 above, you will be able to easily track your results. If you started off with $10,000 and a month later have

$12,245 you'll know that your paper-trading strategy has netted you 22.45 percent in only one month.

Keep notes of your portfolio value each time you calculate it so that you can see not only how your stocks have performed since you started the exercise, but how they have performed from one check to the next.

Keep in mind that you are trying to compare your results not only against your starting value, but also against the market and the underlying sectors in general. If the stock markets have dropped 15 percent since you started the exercise, but your portfolio has dropped only 2 percent, you can know that you're outperforming the markets and therefore doing something right.

Don't forget to take off brokerage commissions for each trade. If you have a stockbroker, check to see how much she would charge you for each transaction, based on the volume, price of shares, and overall cost. Remember that limit orders are usually more expensive than market orders. Make notes of the commissions you took off your portfolio and how you calculated each. Alternatively, you could use a realistic number like $15 per trade if you're not sure what your broker will charge.

Differences between Paper Trading and Real Trading

When you make the jump to trading real money, you may suddenly find that your stocks are not performing as you had anticipated. There are several reasons that may cause this situation:

- Your emotions take over. While you may have been careless and aggressive with imaginary money, your decisions and thought processes will be different once you start using your hard-earned dollars. Paper traders are generally immune to greed, panic, anger, and impatience, but that all changes once they dive in with real money.
- Market activity will be different between the time you tried out a paper-trading strategy and when you start trading actual stocks. While paper trading, the markets may have held up

well, only to crash once you put a few dollars in. Always compare your trading results to the overall markets.

- The rules will be different, especially if you used something like the daily closing price to record your transaction levels. You cannot buy or sell a stock "at the closing price," but instead are subject to intraday volumes and activity. You may even see yourself getting partial fills, such as 1,000 of the 5,000 shares you wanted, because the volume was not great enough at your limit price.
- If you learn nothing else from this book, one thing that I really hope you'll take with you is the need to paper trade. Make some imaginary trades on paper—start now, tonight. Maybe you'll find out that you're no good at picking stocks at all, so even in that case you'll have preserved some capital you may have otherwise lost.

4

Leeds Analysis

WHAT LEEDS ANALYSIS CAN DO

Leeds Analysis is the most widely known method of performing penny stock research. It is designed to find high-quality penny stocks while avoiding the risky ones.

Ninety-five percent of penny stocks fail Leeds Analysis. Only 5 percent are good enough to make the grade, and those that do are more likely to create profits for investors and less likely to suffer downside.

Leeds Analysis looks at just about every factor of a potential investment, such as the:

- Company's situation
- Industry's situation
- Investor interest in the shares
- Volatility levels of the shares
- Risks involved
- Management team
- Possible positive and negative eventualities
- Direction the company is heading
- Goals and vision
- Brand positioning
- Marketing strategy

The result is that Leeds Analysis uncovers penny stocks with:

- Solid foundations
- Good current situations/positions
- Optimistic outlooks
- Proven and expected upside potential
- Momentum in most aspects of their business

Leeds Analysis eliminates the penny stocks that are risky and focuses on quality companies that are undiscovered or undervalued. It reveals penny stocks that are poised to become something big, and those that will experience that growth fast. That's what Leeds Analysis can do for you, just as it has done for tens of thousands of people.

Leeds Analysis is a mix of:

- 80 percent fundamental analysis
- 10 percent technical analysis
- 10 percent Third Level Analysis

Fundamental Analysis

When we perform Leeds Analysis, we start off with the fundamentals. These include any and all factors that can give you an understanding of a company's:

- Past operational results
- Current expectations
- Future outlook

Fundamentals encompass just about every aspect of how a business is operated, what results it has had, and what it hopes to achieve.

Some fundamental factors include, but are not limited to:

- Financial results (income, debt load, costs to produce their product, etc.)
- Financial ratios (debt to equity, price to earnings, etc.)
- Management team
- Lawsuits
- Intellectual property rights
- Industry conditions
- Competition
- Acquisition strategy/acquisition target

A big part of Leeds Analysis involves looking into the financial results of companies. You may have heard of income statements, balance sheets, and cash flow reports. Well, now it's time you learned how much money you can potentially make simply by gaining an understanding of the secrets that the financials reveal.

People get intimidated by looking into company financials, because they believe it to be a lot of complicated math that only an accountant would understand. Don't worry—it's actually simple and much more straightforward than you realize. This is especially true once you learn exactly what to look for and where to find it. For example, you'll be able to know how much money the company owes, how much it is bringing in, and how those figures compare to last year.

If you're thinking about buying shares in ABC Corporation, wouldn't you want to know how much money it makes for each item it sells? Of course you would. As you can probably see, there's nothing difficult or complicated about this. You simply want to get a clear picture of an investment before you risk your money.

Leeds Analysis looks into annual and quarterly financials, which include the:

- Income statement (how much money a company made, and what it cost the company to generate those sales)

- Balance sheet (how much a company has, and how much it owes)
- Cash flow statement (how much money came in and went out)

We are taking a look under the hood. The financial results tell a story about a company, showing you where it has been, what it is capable of, and how well it executes on its business model. The information is powerful and multiplies in usefulness when you compare that information directly against the company's competitors.

When you gain an understanding of a company's financial state, you've taken a significant step in improving your clarity about the value of the shares, and therefore your buying decision.

Once you grasp the financials, the other fundamental aspects of Leeds Analysis are very straightforward. It doesn't take much to assess a company's management team, competition, legal situation, and other fundamental factors.

Some of the factors we'll discuss in this book include, but are not limited to:

- The personal situations of the management team. (Are the CEO and CFO dating? Is the COO a known alcoholic? Are the executives all over 80 years old?)
- Reliance on media coverage. If press relations are a big part of the company's marketing plan, be aware of any major events taking shape that will dominate the airwaves (war, election, etc.), making media coverage for the company harder to come by.
- Barriers to entry. How difficult is it for new competition to enter this market?
- Customer and employee attrition rates. (How many of its customers/employees does the company lose over time?).
- The company's competition analysis projects. (Is it keeping tabs on its competitors, and how is it scoring compared to a year ago? Five years ago?)
- Countermeasures the company employs in reacting to competitors' products/services, marketing campaigns, and promotions.

Trading Tactics: Sentiment

Current investor sentiment refers to how optimistic (or pessimistic) the majority of investors are feeling—in other words, the beliefs and expectations that the majority of people have at the current time.

If everyone thinks the stock market is about to crash, that represents highly negative investor sentiment. If the world seems to be stampeding to throw their money into stocks, and even your great-grandmother is phoning you with her latest stock pick (similar to the environment in which the dot-com bubble was being inflated), then that's highly optimistic sentiment.

Now, here's the important part. Investor sentiment is a *contrarian* indicator. The greater the percentage of people that are optimistic, and the more optimistic those people are, the more likely the market will drop or crash. If everybody expects shares in ABC Inc. to go up, they are highly likely to go down. If 90 percent of investors believe that XYZ Corp. shares are going to collapse, then those same shares are probably going to go higher.

This truth occurs in the stock market for two reasons:

1. Most investors are usually wrong.
2. People act on their beliefs.

The second point that people act on their beliefs, results in traders buying into stocks they expect to go higher, and that buying pressure pushes the shares higher or holds them up. When everybody who thinks the stock will increase in price has bought, and that buying pressure disappears, the shares are usually overvalued and due for a fall.

The same holds true in reverse. When the stock market crashes, and everybody is running for the exits, the mob-mentality selling drives the prices lower. Eventually, the last panicking investor has sold.

At that point, anyone you talk to will have a highly negative outlook about investments. That's when negative sentiment has reached its peak and therefore traders are most likely to be wrong. There

(Continued)

Trading Tactics: Sentiment (*Continued*)

aren't any more sellers, because everyone's sold, but they still believe there is even more downside. Really all that's left are highly under-valued companies that won't go any lower and are about to increase in price.

Use investor sentiment to your advantage. It takes a lot of courage to buy when everyone else is selling, but the harder it becomes for you, the more likely it is that you are making the right move.

Technical Analysis

This is the 10 percent of Leeds Analysis where you look into the trading activity of the shares. You are hoping to gain an understanding of things like buying/selling opportunities, normal trading volumes, expected price volatility, and predictive chart patterns.

Everything to be learned from technical analysis originates from the *trading chart*. Much like fundamental analysis tells a story about the health of the underlying company, technical analysis tells us a story about what prices to buy and sell the shares at, and when to do it.

The technical part of Leeds Analysis will look at aspects such as:

- Investor interest in the shares
- Changes in that interest
- Buying opportunities
- Profit-taking opportunities
- Increases/decreases in volatility
- Price support levels
- Price resistance levels
- Chart patterns indicating potential upcoming price drops/ spikes

Third Level Analysis

The remaining 10 percent of Leeds Analysis is called *Third Level Analysis.* This concept is more abstract than fundamental and technical analysis, but it is an important part of the big picture. Few analysts and newsletter editors perform anything similar to Third Level Analysis, and certainly it's rarely done when average investors are performing their due diligence.

With Third Level Analysis we can't point you to a line on a financial report, or have you look for a pattern on a chart. That is why I say it is an *abstract* concept—there is actually nothing specific to find from one company to the next. You aren't looking for any particular thing; rather you are just looking.

When you find something of importance, you'll know. The best way to give you an understanding of Third Level Analysis is to provide some examples that you may encounter:

- What level of employee poaching and brain-drain is occurring due to actions of their competitors?
- What is the quality and effectiveness of the company's branding?
- How does the company position its product to stand out above the marketing noise in its industry?
- How does the company try to communicate to its prospects, and how are those messages interpreted by potential clients?
- What do customers say about the company's product/service, and what do its competitors say about the same product/service?
- How does the company differentiate itself from competing products and services?

Third Level Analysis is a very broad, abstract topic. However, you probably have a much better understanding of it than you did a few minutes ago.

The previous list is just a sample of some of the ideas that go into Third Level Analysis. Not every point on this list is applicable to every company, nor is it equally important from one company to the next. As well, there are many other important considerations that are not on this list.

As you look deeper and deeper into a company, the important Third Level Analysis issues will pop up and be obvious to you. Until you are actually looking at the details of a company, you can't know which factors require you to pay special attention.

Trading Tactics: Short Selling

Short selling is for when you're betting that the stock price will go down. This is for experienced traders only, and most brokers won't allow you to short sell stocks that trade for less than $5 per share.

With short selling, you sell the shares first, and then have the commitment to buy them back at a later date.

Traders who short a stock are betting that it will decrease in value and that when they go to fulfill their commitment to repurchase the shares they'll be able to do so at a lower price.

Their profits are equal to the difference in price from the original sell to the subsequent buy. If you sold a stock short at $10, and it fell to $8, at which point you bought it back, then you profited $2 per share.

As most brokers don't allow traders to short stocks under a certain threshold price (usually $5 per share), it's very difficult to apply this strategy with penny stocks. This is probably for the best, as I discourage any new or intermediate investors from shorting stocks at any level.

Unlike regular investing, where the most you can lose is 100 percent of your investment, with short selling your losses are unlimited.

For example, if you short a stock at $6.50 and that stock rises to $85.00, you are legally required to buy back the same number of shares you sold short in the first place; 100 shares at $6.50 means you took in $650, but now it will cost you $8,500 to buy them back. You may have had only a few hundred dollars to begin with!

The potential of unlimited losses is not appropriate for most traders. As well, shorting is one of those investment concepts that sounds simple but turns out to be significantly more difficult and costly in practice.

CHAPTER 5

Third Level Analysis

WELCOME TO THIRD LEVEL ANALYSIS

Third Level Analysis is generally conducted after both fundamental and technical research. As such, it was also intended to be included last in *Invest in Penny Stocks*, after the other components of Leeds Analysis. However, we decided to bring it up to the front for a few important reasons.

It's actually with an understanding of the major concepts in Third Level Analysis, such as branding, positioning, and differentiation, that you will be able to uncover many potential investment opportunities. Before you even look into their financial statements, or review the trading chart, you may see their well-branded products flying off the shelves right before your eyes as you walk through the mall.

When a compelling product or service catches your attention, from a Third Level Analysis perspective, it may then be time to apply the fundamental and technical aspects of Leeds Analysis to the company.

As well, unlike the majority of the other aspects of Leeds Analysis, you won't always need a computer, or to be sitting at your office. Rather, you need only pay attention to the marketing approaches of companies you see each day, and watch the world around you.

Third Level Analysis truly has no official rank order. It does not come before or after the rest of Leeds Analysis but rather is a major component of the overall methodology.

 ## Overview

Fundamental analysis considers the strength of a company, and *technical* analysis looks for buying opportunities. The other step is Third Level Analysis and it reviews any miscellaneous and abstract facets of a company that could come into play.

This is just another way in which Leeds Analysis goes beyond other techniques, and why it has been so successful. Third Level Analysis reviews aspects of each stock such as:

- Branding
- Positioning
- Differentiation
- Habits/personal life of management
- Brain drain/employee poaching
- Management accessibility

 ## Branding

Think of Harley Davidson. Lots of companies sell motorcycles, but people gladly join the waiting list for a new Harley because that's the only hog they'll ever consider riding. HD has a stranglehold on the *concept* of the motorcycle, and they reinforce this idea at every brand touch-point—at the dealership, when the bike gets serviced, with television ads, at motorcycle events.

Every company has a certain degree of branding, albeit usually on a lower level than Harley. Picture a small technology start-up. What are its customers saying about the company's software? What are its competitors saying? What was your experience with the company's software? Its customer service? Its prices? Its tech support? These facets all go into the pot, and cook up the company's overall brand experience.

Most people are not very aware of branding, and truly the best branding efforts are meant to go unnoticed. You don't know exactly why you prefer Harley Davidson over Honda Motorcycles, but you just do. While usually going "unseen," branding is a very important factor in any company's success.

Begin to notice branding around you each day. Not just in advertisements, but in all facets of a product or service. Once you become aware, you will start to notice good branding and bad branding. Once you can see that difference, you will have an advantage when performing Leeds Analysis and when making investing decisions.

You want to find companies that have strong branding that:

- Is positive and effective
- Encourages word-of-mouth referrals
- Generates good connotations about the company
- Helps add to the company's market share

Consider the airline industry. Southwest Airlines is an example of bad branding, as the company has spent millions trying to educate people that their planes fly all across America and not just in the Southwest. Their poorly branded name is costly, misleading, and detrimental to the company's success.

Virgin Airlines, on the other hand, is very well branded. The company is associated with the Virgin parent company, a well-known, generally well-liked corporation. Its name is mildly shocking, which helps the company stand out from generic competitors like United and Southwest. It is also known for doing things "better," and in a maverick way.

Here's a quick test to prove the importance of branding: Ask people who have never flown on either Virgin or Southwest which they believed would be the better airline. They would almost always choose Virgin.

Positioning

Indian Motorcycles couldn't compete with Harley in terms of market share, so the company positioned itself as a more expensive, premium bike. An Indian typically costs more than a Harley. If you are looking for something a little higher end than HD, your choice becomes Indian. In positioning itself to capture the market of high-end motorcycle buyers the company has claimed a niche that not even HD will be able to break into.

When most people think of safety in cars, they think about Volvo. This does not mean that Volvo is the safest car. It does mean, however, that consumers whose priorities include safety have an increased likelihood of choosing Volvo. Those same consumers will also be willing to pay a higher price.

All companies are affected by positioning, whether they know it or not. Most CEOs and in fact most marketing and salespeople don't really know about or properly understand positioning. This results in missed opportunities, wasted capital, and loss of market share.

Consider Wal-Mart. The company has positioned itself primarily on price, and no other company can truly compete with it in that regard. At the other end of the spectrum, there are products that position themselves as the most expensive. Consider Lamborghini, Joy (widely known and marketed as the most expensive perfume in the world back in 1930), and the Ritz Carlton. People actually choose the most expensive option often *because* it's the most expensive. Companies that position themselves properly to take advantage of this can really benefit.

An example of poor positioning can be found whenever a company goes against the public perception, or tries to compete head-to-head with a company that already owns a position in the mind of consumers.

Imagine if another retail store tried to compete with Wal-Mart by claiming that it had the absolute lowest prices. A few things would happen in the minds of consumers:

- Some would assume this new company was misleading the public.
- Some would assume that all it sold was junk.
- Some would assume that it had a few products priced lower than Wal-Mart but then would get you with higher prices for the rest of its products.

This new company would start at a major disadvantage. It also would blow its bank account just trying to educate the market that it *does* have quality products at lower prices than Wal-Mart. (Educating a market is the most difficult, most expensive, and most time-consuming thing a company can do. Be warned!)

After all of this cost and effort, even if it had some success (which it wouldn't) teaching people about its store, this retailer still would need to deal with one last cold, hard fact: Even the consumers it *had* educated would still go to Wal-Mart!

Experience
Level 4

Trading Tactics: Hedging

Hedging involves playing two or more sides of a trade in order to reduce overall risk.

For example, you own U.S. dollars as an investment. You could then buy gold, which generally rises when the dollar falls and falls when the dollar rises.

This is a *hedge*, which helps limit the potential loss you might take when an investment drops. It also usually limits the upside you would enjoy if the original investment (the U.S. dollar in this example) performed very well.

Let's say you have holdings in a transportation company that sees its profit margins disappear when fuel prices rise. You may then want to buy shares in an oil production company, because it *benefits* from higher fuel prices.

The two will act in opposite directions to a certain extent. If the price of oil rises, hurting your transport stock, you will at least have gains in your oil stock. When oil prices fall, hurting the oil company, you'll

(Continued)

Trading Tactics: Hedging *(Continued)*

see the transport company benefit. Transportation and oil production companies make an excellent hedge complement.

We encourage hedging for traders with larger portfolios (i.e., $10,000+) when it makes sense to the individual, although it is by no means necessary. Hedging enables penny stock traders to reduce risk while diversifying their exposure.

Hedging is a simple concept, but it can be as complicated as you want to make it. Some hedging strategies get so involved that you could wind up with a chain of six different investments, just to protect every aspect of your approach.

In fact, hedging can take so many different forms and be used for so many different purposes that it could be a book in itself.

I don't suggest that anyone get into highly complicated hedging strategies, but I do believe that simpler, less involved approaches can be very beneficial.

Experience
Level 2

Differentiation

When a market is saturated with competition, differentiation becomes very important. There are hundreds of options for weight loss, or stock picks, or clothes. How do products and services stand out above the noise and thereby make enough money to survive? They need to differentiate and make that difference easily and readily known.

What's the difference between Dom Perignon and other champagnes? Dom is widely known to be very expensive. Therefore, if you want to blow some money in front of your friends, buy a bottle of Dom Perignon.

What's the difference between Google and Yahoo!? Google is a pure-play search engine, meaning that it mainly does search. I understand that it also does maps, news, and more, but early on Google differentiated itself by focusing exclusively on search, and that is part of the reason that it does it the best. It's also the main reason why the public adopted Google so quickly, making it the search engine of choice above several portal-style web sites that had search capabilities as only one of many other features. (You don't want to go to a dentist who also does brain surgery and delivers babies. You want to go to a dentist that is always, and only, a dentist.)

Yahoo, on the other hand, gives you a full community, right on its search page, which includes news, tools, weather, and more. It differentiated itself from Google and other pure-play engines by offering the portal approach. This helped Yahoo! survive Google's perceived superiority in the search game.

By differentiating, both Google and Yahoo! avoided going head-to-head, and instead the two of them gobbled up massive market share from all the other players in the industry. If they had both gone after search only, or both gone portal-style only, they would have spent much more money and resources on marketing, promotion, and development.

Think of it this way: In a small town there might be enough business for three restaurants, but there's only enough customers for one Italian place, one Chinese place, and one steak house. A second steak house would instantly put the future of both steak houses in jeopardy because they weren't differentiated well enough.

In this example, both the Italian and Chinese restaurants' business would be unaffected by the new steak house. Differentiation is the key to survival in any market that is competitive or crowded.

Habits/Personal Life of Management

An alcoholic CEO can run a company into the ground by the time he remembers where he was last night. A mother of five who is expecting a sixth may not make for a good CFO, assuming that the pregnancy and raising the children distract her from the corporate duties. Key managers who routinely take long vacations may demonstrate to you that their level of commitment to the company should be questioned.

While it is difficult to learn everything you would want to know about the management team, you will be able to learn some things.

Publicly traded companies make it known who their management players are, and often give good write-ups on the web site. Failing that, just call the company and ask.

Then you can look deeper into each of them online, perhaps through social networking sites, or doing search engine queries, such as Google news searches, for their names. Also, find out where they worked before and see if that leads you to any more information.

Are they married? Is it marriage number one, or number six? Do they host company parties at their home every second week? Do they have kids, and is it 1, or 12? Are they on vacation every second month? Were they intoxicated at the annual shareholders' meeting? Is one of their favorite hobbies something dangerous, like racing motorcycles?

You might be amazed at some of the stuff you find. You can be sure that with Leeds Analysis, and with an in-depth management search, you will know more about the underlying company than just about every other investor out there.

Brain Drain/Employee Poaching

I've seen this snuff out entire companies. Sometimes a smaller player has all the brains it needs, but can't yet afford to pay very compelling salaries. That's when a bigger competitor with deep pockets swoops in and scoops up all the talent. It gives a competitive advantage to the bigger company, and it also gets the inside knowledge that the employee carries with him to the new job.

At the same time, it makes things very difficult for the smaller company to gain any momentum, especially when it is continually filling holes, training new employees, and paying higher salaries to stem the losses.

Especially in technology companies, look for strong employee loyalty, competitive salaries, and reasons that the key players won't be stolen away. If all key personnel have big ownership stakes in the company, rock-solid non-compete contracts, and confidentiality clauses, they may be less likely to jump ship.

Also take a look at their main competitors, specifically at the employees. Where did most of the staff work before they were at this new job? Was it for the company that you are looking into? Speak to the Investor Relations contact at the competition, and ask her where her employees are mainly coming from. Get an idea if there's some pretty severe employee poaching. Sometimes, especially in technology companies, but potentially in any kind of corporation, brain drain can be running wild.

Trading Tactics: Limiting Losses

The reasons to limit losses are obvious. Of course, don't forget opportunity costs. If you put $1,000 into a stock that goes down 20 percent, not only did you lose $200, but you also lost any potential gains you could have made if that same $1,000 had been invested elsewhere.

Whenever you commit money to one place, you're not only committing to where the money will be, you're committing to where the money won't be.

There are many ways to limit losses when trading stocks:

- Get strong, fundamentally solid companies in the first place by doing Leeds Analysis. Finding the best companies and paying bargain prices for them is the first step to limiting your losses
- *Position sizing* is an important concept. I will go into further detail about position sizing elsewhere in this book, but it is one of the most important ways to limit your losses.
- Paper trading will help you learn the ropes while discovering how to dodge some of the easily avoidable mistakes.
- Diversification is a great way to limit your losses. You don't have all your eggs in one basket. You can diversify by any number of methods or concepts, or even a combination of them. You can diversify by industry, market, geography, market cap, or even the amounts invested per stock. For example, if you had 10 different investments, perhaps they would be from five or six or seven

(Continued)

Trading Tactics: Limiting Losses (*Continued*)

different industry groups, from three different continents, and 10 different market capitalizations.

- Avoid emotional decisions. Don't fall in love with a company; it's just business. If you find yourself losing sleep, trading when you're angry, or stressing out about a stock, then it's not the investment for you.

- Use stop losses. You may find that your broker, especially if you are trading penny stocks, is not very friendly about allowing stop losses. In such a case, simply keep track of your intended stop loss in your head, so that if your stock falls to a certain point, no matter what, you liquidate your position. This prevents further downside for an investment that may be heading toward zero.

- Look for penny stocks with good trading volume. This will help you limit your losses, since you can liquidate your position easily and quickly if required. Good trading volume also demonstrates that the company is more widely followed, and therefore more likely to have strong investor interest.

- Take some profit off the table over time. That way you are proactively limiting any potential losses. If you have a stock that doubles in price, some traders tend to take some of their profit, then let the rest ride.

- Limit orders are an excellent way to curtail your losses. If you are buying with a market order, you wind up getting the best available sell price at that moment. However, especially when dealing with thinly traded penny stocks, market orders can result in traders paying more than they expected. Their very act of buying with a market order drives the price higher. On the other hand, limit orders allow you to choose the maximum price you will pay for the shares, so there will be no surprises.

- Trade on the better markets. There are a lot of problems with the pink-sheets market. You'll generally get better companies, with better reporting requirements, enforcement, regulations, and trading volume on stock exchanges like the OTC-BB (Over-the-Counter Bulletin Board), Nasdaq, AMEX, NYSE, and the Canadian markets like the TMX, and the TMX Venture Exchange.

- How you limit losses and protect your capital really depends on your personal situation, experience level, strategy, and tactics. Some people are playing with a thousand dollars, and don't care if they lose it. They just want the excitement of getting involved

Trading Tactics: Limiting Losses (*Continued*)

with penny stocks, and to take a chance for that investment to become worth much more.

- On the other hand, if you can't afford to lose your investment, your strategy for limiting losses will be much different. In fact, if you can't afford to risk your capital, your real approach should be "investment abstinence!"

- Overall, the very best way to limit losses is never purchase any stock until you feel absolutely comfortable with it. Know why you are investing in this company. Understand where you expect the share price to go, and how fast. Be clear about why the company is going to do well. Know at what point you want to take your profits. Take full responsibility for whatever happens, and don't buy unless you feel very confident and comfortable with your decision.

Call the Company

This is the simplest, most powerful tool to give you an investment advantage, and yet the vast majority don't do it. Call the company, ask questions, make sure you understand management's strategy and outlook, and see what to expect in the coming months.

Just about every publicly traded company has a designated Investor Relations (IR) contact. This person's job is to speak to current and prospective investors and answer any questions they may have.

You might be surprised how much you can learn about a company, and how quickly. These gems of insight could never have been gleaned through reading the financials, press releases, or the company web site.

So why do so few take advantage of the IR contacts? My guess would be that people aren't sure of what to ask, or they don't feel entitled to do so. Maybe they are concerned that they might sound stupid. I can't really know, but I will tell you that it makes a lot of sense to make a quick 15-minute phone call to get an idea of the prospects and direction of a company that you're about to invest in. Even better, follow up once or twice over the following year, checking in just to make sure everything is still on track with the business plan.

Before you make that call, you should:

- Know what you intend to ask (a list of good questions follows).
- Know with whom you are speaking (name, title).
- Have a thorough knowledge of the company.

You shouldn't ask things that you could have just as easily learned from the company's public releases, financials, or web site materials. That's just being considerate for the time of the Investor Relations contact.

When you are ready to take it a step further, you should even have similar conversations with the IR contacts of the company's closest competitors. Don't say you are calling to see if you should invest in the first company, but rather pretend to be an interested investor in this second company's shares.

Here are some good questions:

- You've had increasing revenues over the past couple of years. Do you expect this trend to continue, and what will be the key drivers to make that happen?
- Your employee count has gone up from 10 to 20 in the last year. How many of that original 10 are still with the company?
- Of your 8 salesmen, how many have been with the company for less than a year?
- If the company has $1 million in excess capital, would that go toward R&D, paying down debt, or elsewhere?
- Your competitor is putting out press releases about its upcoming launch of its newest technology. What do you know about that technology and how will your company respond to its release?

CHAPTER 6

Fundamental Analysis

THE IMPORTANCE OF FUNDAMENTALS

Fundamental analysis considers and interprets just about every factor that impacts a company. This represents 80 percent of the focus of Leeds Analysis and is the most important part of finding high-quality penny stocks with great upside potential.

It's important, if you don't like a penny stock once you start to look deeper into it or you find even one or two warning signs, that you drop it and move on to the next opportunity. Be demanding. This will save you time and increase your likelihood of finding those really good opportunities. Don't get bogged down doing research into companies that have things going against them; as soon as it becomes clear that they will fail Leeds Analysis, you should move on to the next opportunity.

The idea is that you find a few really compelling penny stocks that, in your opinion, pass Leeds Analysis and could multiply in value several times over. Some of these penny stocks absolutely balloon in price and can make thousands of dollars out of hundreds.

When performing Leeds Analysis on the fundamentals of a penny stock, here is how we proceed:

- Look at the financial results (gives an understanding of the operational situation).
- Look for trends compared to previous quarters and years.
- Generate financial ratios (gives much deeper understanding).
- Compare financial ratios to previous quarters and years.
- Explore other fundamental considerations (those not related to the financials).

When you look through the financial results of a company, and its financial ratios, you may not be sure whether the numbers you are seeing are strong or weak, especially if you're a newer investor.

For example: Is a revenue level of $150 million good? Well, that depends. How big is the company? What are its costs? How does $150 million compare to its revenues last year?

Is $300 million too much debt? Maybe; maybe not. You can't know right away, but as you proceed through Leeds Analysis and continually keep getting a bigger picture, you will get clarity. You will know things about the company that help you make the right decisions at the right time while other investors just trade based on newspaper articles and gut feelings.

There are also differences among various industries. To be considered strong, a technology company will have very different numbers than a biotech company. For example, it is rare for a biotech to be making any profit at all, while a utility company will generally be profitable. A high-growth company in a high-growth industry can have a share price that is 100 times its earnings, while the share price of a company in a low-growth industry should be closer to 10 times earnings.

Think of it like a jigsaw puzzle. You look at a piece and aren't quite sure where it fits. Without the lid of the box, you probably wouldn't even be sure what the picture on the puzzle is supposed to be. However, as you fit more pieces together, eventually you're going to see the big picture.

You'll gain all the clarity you need by:

- Comparing the company's numbers to previous quarters and annual results
- Comparing the company's numbers to direct competitors and the overall industry
- Using financial ratios
- Comparing those ratios to competitors and the overall industry
- Using your own logic (e.g., revenues of $1 million with expenses of $20 million is really quite a problem!)

You will significantly power-up your Leeds Analysis when you compare a company to its competitors and to its overall industry. Only through comparison will you achieve the greatest level of clarity.

Consider a company that has been growing by 25 percent each year. That sounds pretty good. However, it's not as good if all its competitors grew by over 70 percent in that same timeframe. This illustrates the value of performing Leeds Analysis not only on the penny stock you like, but on other relevant companies as well.

Financial Results

A company's financial results tell a story. You'll quickly get an idea of how solid the penny stock is, how effective the company's business model will be, and whether the shares might be ready to spike in price.

The financials are put together in three reports:

1. **Income statement:** how much money the company made, and what it cost to make that happen
2. **Balance sheet:** what the company owns, and what it owes
3. **Cash flow statement:** money coming in and going out, and the change in cash since the last statement

(*Note:* You can gain access to a company's financials for free online at dozens of web sites like Yahoo! Finance and Market Watch.)

While it can seem like an intimidating or confusing task, rest assured that it is much easier (and more fun) than you probably think. I will oversimplify the ideas for our purposes. If you want to get more in depth with financial analysis, there are many good tutorial web sites you can visit to learn more.

For simplicity, most financial reports display numbers in thousands, where $10,540 actually represents $10,540,000. Sometimes the numbers are displayed in millions. Either way, there will be a note at the top or beginning of the financials clarifying this.

There are often different names for the same thing. For example, *sales* means the exact same thing as *revenue*. Luckily, while different financial statements might have different names for various items, they all follow a similar setup. For example, one company might have separate amounts for research and development expenses, administrative expenses, and non-recurring expenses, while another company might combine all of those and just call it *operating expenses.*

Experience Level 5

The Income Statement

The first step in Leeds Analysis is to go directly to the financial reports, starting with the income statement. This tells you how much money the company made, what its expenses were, and whether it is operating profitably or at a loss.

The income statement is laid out as follows:

- **Sales** (how much money the company brought in)
- **Cost of sales** (expenses to fulfill those sales)
- **Gross profit** (profits from sales after cost of sales)
- **Operating expenses** (all other costs in addition to cost of sales)
- **Net profit** (how much the company made after all costs)

The first line, called either *sales* or *revenues,* displays how much money the company made. Whether it produces a product, provides a service, or does both, all of its income from those activities is included.

The next few lines generally include various items, such as cost of sales, which reveals how much it cost the company to produce its product or provide its service. If it made $10 million, and its cost of sales is $6 million, it has a gross profit of the difference, which is $4 million. The greater the company's sales are compared to its cost of sales, the better.

In the next few lines, the income statement factors in operating expenses. These are things like research and development of new products, administrative salaries, general costs like rent and heating the facility/office, and so forth.

This all adds up to the company's *total operating expenses*. Take this amount off of the gross profit and you have your *net profit*, which is simply the money left over after all operations.

Pretty simple, right?

Let's take a closer look at the items you'll see on an income statement, and review a simplified example. (See Figure 6.1.)

- Income represents money the company generated by selling its products and services.
- Cost of goods is the costs related to producing products or providing services.
- Gross profit margin is the difference between income and cost of goods. Gross profit margin can be expressed in dollars ($525,000), or as a percentage of revenue (gross profit margin = 20%).
- Operating expenses include all overhead and labor expenses associated with the operations of the business, such as research and development costs, administrative, and advertising.
- Total expenses are the sum of cost of goods and operating expenses.
- Net profit is the gross profit margin after deducting operating expenses.

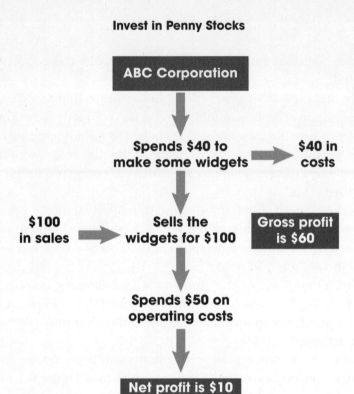

Figure 6.1 Simplified Income Statement

- Depreciation reflects the decrease in value of capital assets used to generate income. For example, a brand-new $5,000 computer isn't worth as much a year later, and even less each year after that.
- Earnings before interest and taxes shows how much profit the company made, but interest payments and corporate tax obligations have not yet been factored in.
- Interest includes interest payable for short-term and long-term debt.
- Taxes includes all taxes on the business.
- Net profit after tax, also called the *bottom line*, shows the company's real profit.

Table 6.1 illustrates a simplified example of the income statement of a fictional company.

Table 6.1   Fictional Income Statement

Sample Fictional Company – Income Statement
Fiscal Year Ended April 30, 2009 (all amounts in thousands)

Operating Revenue (Income)	**100,000**	= this is their total sales
Cost of Goods Sold (COGS)	40,000	= cost to create the product
Gross Profit Margin	**60,000**	= revenue less cost of goods
Research + Development	5,000	= money spent on R + D
Selling, General, and Administrative	10,000	= costs of SG + A
Advertising	15,000	= advertising costs
Operating Expenses	30,000	= total of above three items
Total Expenses	70,000	= COGS + operating expenses
Net Profit (EBITDA)	**30,000**	= revenue less total expenses
Depreciation	1,000	= depreciation expense
Earnings before Interest + Taxes (EBIT)	**29,000**	= net profit less depreciation
Interest	500	= interest payments on debt
Taxes	500	= income taxes paid
Net Profit (after Taxes)	**28,000**	= how much they really made

Trading Tactics: Pinpoint Investing

The more you diversify, the closer your returns will come to the overall market average. This is as true for penny stocks as for any other investment vehicle. Buy a little of everything and you get what everybody is getting.

The problem with "what everybody is getting" is that it's not life-changing, not exciting, and not going to produce any tangible result for your investment efforts. Go ahead, make 7 percent on your money for the next three years and tell me how it all works out for you.

I would rather pass on diversification. I practice something different with my personal penny stock investments, something that is quite the opposite. I call my methodology, "Pinpoint Investing."

Simply put, I will generally be invested in from six to nine penny stocks at any one time. No matter how much capital I bring to bear, I rarely go over nine individual penny stocks.

(Continued)

Trading Tactics: Pinpoint Investing (*Continued*)

I make sure I feel strongly about each company's prospects, know the ins and outs of its operations, follow its growth plan, and put it through Leeds Analysis of course!

Then, I get involved with these companies in a meaningful way. I don't get nervous putting six-figure amounts into my choices, because I know that they are quality companies with tremendous upside potential.

If I have fresh money to invest, I look first to those shares that I already own. Generally, I put that new money into one of my current holdings, buying more shares in the handful of penny stocks that are already in my portfolio.

Most people look to completely new stocks when they have money to invest. I don't blame them, though, because everybody on TV and the newspapers is screaming at us to *diversify*.

When it comes to penny stocks, that shouting gets even worse: "They're risky, so lower your risk by diversifying. Better yet, don't even go near penny stocks. Even better than that, buy these mutual funds—you may make eight percent!"

You know what? That whole "avoid-risk" topic doesn't fly with investors like it used to, because many blue-chip stocks and most mutual funds are trading so much lower than a few years ago. People trying to avoid risk have wound up losing a lot of money in recent years, in so-called "safe" equities, like Microsoft, General Motors, Citibank, Bear Stearns, and others.

You will almost always do better with your penny stock investments by keeping a watchful, interested, and knowledgeable eye on a small portfolio than you will by buying a little bit of everything.

The Balance Sheet

The balance sheet tells you what a company owns and what it owes. It breaks all items down between:

- **Assets** (cash, investments, real estate, factories, etc.)
- **Liabilities** (debt, accounts payable, mortgages, etc.)

The balance sheet also divides assets and liabilities between:

- **Current** (items accessible or due within the next year)
- **Long term** (items accessible or due, but not for a year or more)

For example, cash in the bank would be a current asset, since the company would have easy and quick access to the money if it needed it. On the other hand, a factory that the company owns would be considered a long-term asset since it might take years to sell if the company decided to liquidate it.

To provide a similar example from the liability side, picture a company with a $10 million mortgage. If payments of $400,000 will be due over the next 12 months, then that $400,000 will be treated as a current liability. The remaining $9,600,000 is considered a long-term liability since that part of the debt isn't due within the next 12 months.

The balance sheet is laid out as follows:

Assets (what the company owns and has):
- **Current assets** (accessible within the next year or less)
- **Long-term assets** (not easily accessible within the next year)

Total assets (the total of all current and long-term assets)

Liabilities (what the company is committed to paying and what it owes):
- **Current liabilities** (to be paid in 12 months or less)
- **Long-term liabilities** (due in a year or more)

Total liabilities (the total of all current and long-term liabilities)

You can see how a review of the balance sheet would give you a good picture of a company's financial strength. A penny stock with no long-term debt, very low liabilities, and very high assets is well positioned to operate. Alternatively, a company that owes (liabilities) as much as it has (assets) is in a very tough situation. (See Table 6.2.)

Current assets are items of value that the company could easily use immediately (or relatively soon). Current assets can come into

Table 6.2 Fictional Balance Sheet

Sample Fictional Company – Balance Sheet
> Fiscal Year Ended April 30, 2009 (all amounts in thousands)

ASSETS		= what they own
Current Assets		
Cash	50	= money in accounts
Short-term Investments	25	= can be liquidated quickly
Accounts Receivable	25	= money owed for work done
Inventory	100	= value of current inventory
Loans Receivable	5	= expected to be repaid soon
Prepaid Expenses	5	= early payments for services
Total Current Assets	**210**	= total of all above items
Long Term Assets		= long term, less liquid assets
Land	500	
Buildings	1,000	
Equipment	200	
Less Accumulated Depreciation	(100)	= decreases in value of assets
Net Long Term Assets	**1,600**	(depreciation is treated as a negative number, so is subtracted from assets above)
Intangible Assets		
Trade Names	300	= value of brand names
Total Intangible Assets	**300**	
Total Assets	**2,310**	= sum of current & long term assets
LIABILITIES		= what they owe
Current Liabilities		
Accounts Payable	10	= outstanding invoices
Salaries Payable	40	= owed to employees
Current Portion of Long Term Debt	50	= due within current year
Taxes Payable	10	= due within current year
Total Current Liabilities	**110**	= sum of all current liabilities
Long Term Liabilities		= owed in a year or more
Long Term Debt	1,000	= bonds, credit lines, etc.
Lease Obligations	50	= future lease payments
Mortgage on Factory	150	= mortgage on property
Total Long Term Liabilities	**1,200**	
Total Liabilities	**1,310**	= current + long liabilities

play to meet the day-to-day financial expenses of the company's operations.

Some examples of current assets include, but are not limited to:

- Cash in the bank
- Not-yet-deposited cash, checks, money orders
- Accounts receivable

Unlike current assets, the value of long-term assets could not be cashed out quickly in order to pay the company's expenses. A long-term asset like a factory does have a lot of value, but it would need to be sold before that cash value would ever be realized or used to fund the operations of the company.

Examples of long-term assets include, but are not limited to:

- Equipment
- Furnishings
- Real estate
- Tools, machinery
- Intellectual property

Current liabilities are expenses and amounts owed by the company to others that are due within 12 months or less. Unlike long-term liabilities, which do not have to be paid within the next year, the clock is ticking with current liabilities.

Examples of current liabilities include, but are not limited to:

- Accounts payable
- Short-term loans
- Dividend payments to be made
- Interest payable
- Current portion of long-term debt that is due now

Long-term liabilities are expenses and amounts owed by the company that are not due within the next 12 months.

Examples of long-term liabilities include, but are not limited to:

- Loans
- Bank debt due beyond 12 months
- Mortgages
- Long-term contractual obligations
- Debentures (debt instruments such as IOUs)

The balance sheet reveals a great deal about any company. Will the company survive long? Does it have the funds to buy out its competition? Does it have the capital to expand its research and development efforts? Might it need to raise more money in the near future or take on more debt?

I'm sure you can imagine that getting a clear picture of a company's balance sheet is a major step in predicting the health and risk of the underlying penny stock. You want to look for those corporations that have lots of cash and current assets, without a lot of current liabilities. You should be scared off by companies that have a big debt position, especially if it's close to, or greater than, their total assets.

Picture a company with $30 million in current assets and $10 million in current liabilities. Looks pretty good, because for every dollar it needs to pay out in the next year or less, it's got $3 to cover it. That is a strong short-term (current) asset position.

However, what if you looked further down the balance sheet and found that the company had only $1 million in long-term assets, but had $400 million in long-term debt? It has taken on massive expenses through loans and mortgages that it hasn't had to pay for yet. It has survived this way so far, but unfortunately for this company, there's a train wreck coming.

The thing about long-term debt is that it generates interest and principle payments, both of which add to the current liabilities line item. On top of this, as the months pass, more and more of the long-term debt actually becomes due within a year, and therefore that portion of the debt now transitions from a long-term liability to a current liability. In other words, a small part of that big loan needs to be paid soon, and more and more "small parts" will become due as the months tick past.

In the example given, I'd expect to see the current liabilities number balloon as interest started building up and outstanding debt came closer to being due. Given the huge total debt of $410 million ($400 long term, $10 current), compared to the total assets of $31 million ($1 long term, $30 current), this company is actually worth negative $379 million.

Assets:	**$ 31 million**
Liabilities:	**$410 million**
Shareholder's equity:	**(–$379 million)**

You should also expect that deficit to grow, as the interest payments to float the debt will crush a company that only has $31 million in assets.

This may seem like an extreme example, but in the penny stock world you'll run into lots of companies that are this bad or worse. This is especially true with those that have a wonderful "story" behind the stock, since that story excites investors and makes them overlook the fundamentals while they drive the share price up to ridiculous levels.

Staying with the numbers from the previous example, let's look at the story this company is touting. Perhaps it is working on a cure for cancer. It has already spent $400 million to find that cure and is telling people that it is close. You hear rumors about the company, like it is about to:

- Get FDA approval, or . . .
- Start taking patients, or . . .
- Team up with a major company, or . . .
- Get bought out by an industry goliath, and so forth.

With a balance sheet like that, the *story* is the only thing holding the share price up. The real value of the shares is near zero (actually less than zero), but you'll often see a company just like this trading at a couple bucks a share!

Take Sirius Satellite Radio, for example. The company was sitting on $1 billion in long-term debt, with a few hundred million in revenues, and the share price kept creeping higher. Eventually, of course, shares of Sirius came crashing down to earth, wiping out the value of the investment that so many uneducated investors had made.

The worst part is that people who don't know a lot about investing, and almost certainly don't know how to read the financials, get roped into fundamentally brutal companies like these. Someone hears from a friend that "ABC is about to get FDA approval," and so he buys up a couple thousand dollars' worth of shares. Since the friend didn't review the financials, this story will not end well for him.

The balance sheet, combined with what you learned from the income statement, paints a good picture of the underlying financial strength of a penny stock. However, there is one more aspect that will round out that picture even more. You've heard it: "Cash is king." Well, the cash flow statement will help you separate the kings from the peasants.

Experience Level 5

The Cash Flow Statement

Companies keep track of changes in their money from one period to the next by way of the cash flow statement. All cash generated or used is reported in the following categories:

- **Operating activities**—the effect on cash due to operations, which were the items reported on the income statement.

- **Investing activities**—reports the purchase and sale of long-term investments such as real estate properties, plant, and equipment.
- **Financing activities**—reports the issuance and repurchase of the company's bonds and stock, as well as any dividend payments.
- **Supplemental information**—reports significant items that did not involve cash, as well as income taxes and interest paid.

If you had $20 in your wallet, bought a $5 lunch, and found a quarter on the street, you'd end up with $15.25. That's your personal cash flow statement for the day.

There are a lot of expenses and sources of income beyond the numbers that you see on the income statement. For example, if the corporation issues more shares to raise $8 million, you'll see those dollars listed on the cash flow statement.

After taking into account all the various factors affecting the company's cash position, you'll get a clear idea whether it is up or down overall. Consider this example: A company that made record revenues and earnings looks to be in good shape, but then when you take the cash flow account, you realize that it is actually down $73 million from the previous year. (Perhaps they got hit by foreign exchange rate changes, or made a big investment into some ridiculous product). By reviewing the cash flow, you knew to avoid this company while other investors bought into the company's revenue and earnings successes and probably would be scratching their heads as the shares sank.

Some examples of cash flow items include, but are not limited to:

- Effects of financings or stock offerings
- Dividends paid out
- Adjustments for changes in foreign exchange rates
- Capital expenditures
- Investments
- Borrowings

The line items you'll commonly see on the cash flow statement include the following:

- **Cash** refers to cash on hand.
- **Cash sales** represent sales for which payment has been received.
- **Receivables** represents income owed to the business from sales that are yet to be collected.
- **Other income** is money from investments, interest on loans held by the company, and any asset liquidations.
- **Total income** is the sum of cash, cash sales, receivables, and other income.
- **Material/merchandise** is the value of unused raw materials, merchandise inventory, or supplies that the company can still use to provide products and services.
- **Direct labor** is the labor requirement to manufacture a product or perform a service.
- **Overhead** is all fixed and variable expenses required for the business to operate.
- **Marketing/sales** is salaries, commissions, and other direct costs associated with the marketing and sales departments.
- **R&D (research and development)** is labor expenses required to support the research and development operations.
- **G&A (general and administrative)** is labor expenses required to support the general and administrative functions.
- **Taxes** are all taxes (except payroll) paid to government institutions.
- **Capital** represents the capital requirements to obtain equipment needed to generate income.
- **Loan payments** are the total of payments made to reduce long-term debt.
- **Total expenses** are the sum of material, direct labor, overhead expenses, marketing, sales, R&D, G&A, taxes, capital, and loan payments.

- **Cash flow** is the difference between total income and total expenses. On the subsequent cash flow statement, this amount is carried over as that period's beginning cash.
- **Cumulative cash flow** is the difference between current cash flow and cash flow from the previous period.

Table 6.3 is a simplified example of what a balance sheet might look like and what line items it includes.

Picture a company that earned $1 million dollars. Then you look deeper, and find that it raised $2 million from issuing and selling stock on the open market. All told, that is a net increase in cash of $3 million.

Table: 6.3   Fictional Cash Flow Statement

Sample Fictional Company – Cash Flow Statement
Fiscal Year Ended April 30, 2009 (all amounts in thousands)

Cash	10	= Cash on hand
Cash Sales	60	= sales that have been paid for
Receivables	30	= sales not yet paid for
Other Income	10	= miscellaneous
Total Income	**110**	= sum of above items
Material / Merchandise	10	= unused material or supplies
Direct Labor	20	= labor to use these supplies
Overhead	5	= heat, electricity, phones, etc.
Marketing / Sales	25	= costs for sales department
Research and Development	10	= costs for R + D
General & Administrative	15	= costs for G + A
Taxes	5	= taxes paid
Capital	10	= needed to create any income
Loan Payments	0	= paying down debts
Total Expenses	**100**	= sum of above costs
Cash Flow	10	= total income less expenses
Cumulative Cash Flow	5	= change from last statement

However, what if that company had paid out $3 million in dividends. In that case, it actually merely broke even from a cash flow perspective (generated $3 million total, paid out $3 million).

In this purposely simplified example, the cash flow statement revealed that:

- The company benefited current shareholders by paying out cash dividends.
- It hurt current shareholders by issuing more shares (which dilutes the value of the stock).
- It is no better or worse off (in terms of cash) than the previous year.

Generally, on a cash flow statement you want to see:

- Items that add to the overall cash flow
- Improvements (increases) in these positive items from year to year
- Few items that detract significantly from overall cash flow
- Improvements (decreases) in these negative items from year to year
- A net positive increase in cash from one year to the next

The cash flow statements help:

- Accounting personnel. (Can the company pay what it owes?)
- Potential investors. (Is the company generating or losing cash?)
- Creditors and lenders. (Can the company pay us back?)
- Customers, employees, and contractors. (Will we get paid when it's due?)

You will always have various items on the cash flow statement. However, the ones that have a big impact (e.g., items that have an effect of millions of dollars) need to be investigated further. In some cases, it's fine when a company spends $100 million on capital expenditures, but other times this could be disastrous. When performing Leeds Analysis, look into the significant numbers on the cash flow statement and make sure that they make sense, are moving in the right direction, and are advancing the company forward.

Good Numbers

What is a "good" number to see on the financial results? Should a technology company have higher revenues than it is currently achieving? Should that biotech be spending so much on research and so little on advertising? These are the types of questions that have no hard rules, but there are some general guidelines.

Taken in a vacuum, a number is meaningless: $1.3 million in revenues may be good or bad. For a startup in its first year, such a number might be great, but if we're talking about General Motors, that same number would be a disaster. Thus, every number you look at needs to be considered in relation to:

- The company's competitors
- Its industry
- The previous quarterly report
- The same quarter from the prior year
- The previous years

Is the company growing from year to year? Is its pace of growth slowing down? Do its competitors make similar products for less but sell them for more? Is its debt load much greater than that of bigger companies in the field?

These are just samples of the types of questions that you'll answer as you breeze through the company's (and its competitors') financial results. Don't get discouraged if it sounds like a lot of work, because it really isn't that bad. Once you've gotten familiar with the process and are used to reading the reports, it starts coming very easily and quickly. Besides, it can be a lot of fun, and the fact that it will probably help you make money is just gravy.

Table 6.4 Possible Financial Ratios by Industry Group

Industry	% ROS	% ROA	Quick Ratio	Current Ratio
Accommodation-Food Services	9.75	10.04	0.82	1.14
Administrative-Support-Waste Mgmt	7.68	12.14	0.93	1.25
Agriculture-Forestry-Fishing-Hunting	9.43	12.03	0.90	1.52
Art-Entertainment-Recreation	13.56	16.19	0.89	1.25
Construction	7.07	15.07	0.91	1.69
Eductional Services	12.48	17.99	1.05	1.41
Finance Insurance	17.89	1.91	0.35	0.82
Health Care-Social Assistance	7.96	7.29	0.88	1.14
Information	12.41	4.29	0.71	0.99
Holding Companies	18.9	1.26	0.57	0.77
Manufacturing	11.48	7.96	0.88	1.17
Mining	21.05	12.85	1.17	1.50
Other Services	7.17	13.19	1.41	2.02
Professional-Scientific-Technical	9.7	14.57	0.94	1.22
Real Estate-Rental-Leasing	16.94	10.10	1.15	1.55
Retail Trade	4.29	10.21	0.48	1.36
Transportation-Warehousing	6.72	8.11	0.88	1.14
Utilities	6.38	2.83	0.54	0.99
Wholesale-Retail Trade	4.24	8.98	0.64	1.43

To give you a better idea of the ratios you might expect to see, Table 6.4 demonstrates the variations in financial ratios among industry groups. Keep in mind that this type of data takes a few years to collect and report. Industries fluctuate significantly from month to month and therefore expectations for their financial ratios will also be volatile. For example, a quick ratio of 1.10 for the educational services industry might be strong one year but actually be considered very weak another year if the overall sector suddenly had a much stronger ratio of 1.40 on average.

Percent ROS: return on sales ratio, expressed as a percentage
Percent ROA: return on assets ratio, expressed as a percentage

Quick ratio: current assets (less inventories) divided by current liabilities

Current ratio: current assets divided by current liabilities

The numbers listed in the table are averages for their overall industry sector, from recent history. However, by the time you read Table 6.4, these industry averages will have already changed. The purpose of this table is simply to give you an idea of the kinds of discrepancies you'll see among industries.

Look at the difference in return on sales (ROS) between real estate (16.94) compared to the wholesale sector (4.24). Given this scenario, a wholesale company with an ROS of 8.00 would actually be very strong, but a real estate company with a similar ROS of 8.00 would be considered very weak.

In other words, each company's industry must be taken into account when performing Leeds Analysis. By comparing stocks from different industry groups, you're comparing apples to oranges. You need to compare apples to apples. The only way to do this is by contrasting any company against its competitors in the same sector, as well as against the average for its underlying industry.

Accounting Magic

Corporate financials are sometimes (always) subject to accounting tricks of the trade. This is legal and commonplace, but it can become confusing or misleading to the investors.

Accounting magic is not dishonest, nor is it misleading to industry professionals. The purpose is simply to help the company in various ways, for example, by saving on taxes. It only becomes an issue when investors get confused or misunderstand the true results that the company achieved.

Now, we're not talking about "cooking the books," where executives lie to make their company look better. There is actually little you can do to avoid this, which has been evidenced many times in the past with high-profile cases like Bre-X Minerals, Enron, and more recently the $50 billion Madoff scandal. In these situations, even high-level, professional analysts were completely unaware of the fraud until it was in the news.

In the case of Bre-X, the insiders sprinkled gold on their core samples, so the results showed they had stumbled onto the world's largest gold deposit. Not much you can do about dishonesty like that, and there is nothing you'll find in this book that can ensure you never get played by some terrible CEO.

Instead, we will be focusing here on the legal side of reporting financial results in their best light. This is called "accounting magic," and is the common practice of treating certain items (expenses, payments) in ways that are better for the company. This is done to:

- Make the financial results look stronger.
- Defer or minimize tax payments.
- Write off more costs.
- Create the appearance of growth, improving financials, or positive momentum.

For example, I once saw a $20,000 purchase of an Internet property treated as "office supplies" when it was expensed. Other times, when money is wasted these lost dollars get swept under the carpet by attributing them to "research and development." The R&D figure might be $12.5 million, but often only perhaps $11 million of that was actually used for pure R&D.

These are just some examples, but know that there are hundreds of different ways that accounting magic can come into play. You do not need to fear it, because all income and expenses a company incurs need to be added somewhere on the financials, and how each item should be treated is open for debate. It gets really complicated, and accountants have a lot of options about how they will treat various situations. There really are a lot of gray areas.

For example, an accountant may be faced with the choice of treating a payment to the CEO as a salary, or as a bonus. One way saves the company $40,000 in income taxes, while the other way saves the CEO $70,000 in personal taxes. The accountant's decision will alter the final numbers on the company's financials, affecting the reported salaries, bonus levels, and taxes payable for the corporation.

What percentage of a new computer system should be treated as a capital expense in the year it gets purchased, and what percentage should be offset as a cost to amortize over the coming years? You do not need to understand all this; just be aware that if you are a newer investor, or basically not an accountant, then read between the lines of the fiscal reports. Take the numbers with a grain of salt. If you see any item in the financials that confuses you or doesn't make sense, call the company's CFO and have her give you a full explanation.

Trends in Financial Results

The most important aspect of financial results is their trends. For example, what does a revenue number like $2 million really mean? Well, it means a lot more when you compare it to the previous year of $1 million, and the year before that with revenues of $100,000. You can see a trend of increasing revenues.

Need to Know: Each company's fiscal year starts on a date decided by the company. Each fiscal year is made up of four quarters, with each quarter representing a three-month period. If a company's year-end is December 31, its Q1 runs from January 1 to the last day in March. Q2 would run from April 1 until the last day in June, and so on.

Thus, if a company's year starts on February 1, then its:

- Q1 would run from February 1 to the last day of April (Feb., Mar, April).
- Q2 would run from May 1 to the last day of July (May, June, July).

- Q3 would run from August 1 to the last day of October (Aug., Sept., Oct.).
- Q4 would run from November 1 to the last day of January (Nov., Dec., Jan.).

Each year the company will also compile the results of all four quarters and provide the results as its annual financials, which demonstrate how it performed for the entire year.

Most companies report their financial results about four to six weeks after the quarter end date. There are regulations imposed by the stock exchanges that sanction companies that fail to issue their financial results in a timely fashion.

There are three timeframes to financial results that you can use to uncover the trends:

1. Previous results (last quarter, same quarter last year, previous years)
2. Current results (most recent filing)
3. Upcoming expectations (company issued guidance, or estimates of analysts)

If you are reviewing a company's most recent quarterly financials, you'll want to compare them to:

- The previous quarter
- The same quarter from the previous year

For example, you are looking into the Q3 results for ABC Inc. You want to know how the company compares to the previous three-month period, which in this example would be its Q2. Reviewing the previous results will tell you a lot about its progress and momentum.

However, you also want to compare the results to the same quarter from the previous year to account for seasonality. Therefore, if you are reviewing a company after its Q4 results, also look at its Q3 results and the previous year's Q4.

For example, if the penny stock in question operates a ski hill, you'd see a major increase in revenues from the fall quarter to the winter quarter. Yet, what if you look back to the previous year and realize that the revenues from the previous winter were much higher?

Most businesses have a seasonal effect to some degree, so comparing similar quarters will really help you get a proper picture of the merits of a company.

The next step is to compare the most recent annual financials to previous annual reports. This gives you a more complete picture. It is important to compare year-over-year results because it eliminates effects of seasonality and provides a longer term, more complete view.

After considering the past and current quarters and annuals, you can add to your understanding by looking ahead. If you know beforehand what kind of financial results a company may release, you stand to profit handsomely from your investing. You can get this forward-looking information in any one of three ways:

1. **Calculate estimates yourself.** This is a lot of work, but I would recommend it for experienced investors.
2. **Review analyst estimates.** If a company has analyst estimates, it will be available on sites like Yahoo.com. The more analysts, the more you can trust the data.
3. **Company guidance.** Often a company issues guidance, with expected revenue and earnings ranges for the upcoming fiscal period(s). Generally corporate guidance is pretty accurate, since there are legal consequences when management intentionally misleads investors. Just remember that the guidance can change on any day if the management team realizes that their opinions are off. As well, companies get surprised all the time when they calculate their financials, either seriously exceeding or missing their previously issued guidance.

Guidance (and analyst expectations) can be a tricky thing. When investors are prepared to hear a certain number, the stock trades as if that result is already "baked into the pie."

For example, ABC Inc. is widely expected by analysts to report record revenues of $38 million, blowing away its previously reported $21 million. These analyst expectations are freely and publicly available through sites like Yahoo! Finance. The stock price starts trending upward.

A few weeks later, the management issues guidance that they expect revenues of $35 to $41 million. The stock price balloons further.

Then a few weeks later they calculate and report their results: total revenues of $32 million, shy of the $38 million everyone expected. The stock crashes back down in price. So, despite significantly beating their previous results of $21 million, the shares slump in price with the release of the financials.

Investors and analysts were looking for and expecting a higher number. The anticipation pushed the shares higher, and the actual number did not justify the increased stock price.

Logically, you would think that the company is growing fast, going from $21 million in revenue to $32 million, so its shares must be a good purchase. However, the time to buy would have been before and during the very early anticipation, rather than once the shares had already started their price increase.

Pay attention to the dates of when a company is expected to report financial results. You may want to avoid buying (or selling) shares immediately before they report, because you never know what might happen. Sometimes it can work out well for you; other times it can go badly. Be alert with reporting dates, and keep in mind that this is when surprises in the financials can really move stock prices (in either direction).

Financial Ratios

Financial ratios are very simple yet highly valuable calculations that can really tell you a lot about a company. If you learn to calculate a few of the main ratios yourself, or more likely you use a web site like Yahoo! Finance, which provides them for you, then your trading decisions will be much more informed.

The most common financial ratio, which you've probably heard of before, is *price/earnings*, most widely known as the *P/E ratio*. It is as simple as it looks. You divide the price of the shares by the company's latest annual earnings. A company that trades at $10 a share, and last year had earnings of $2, will have a P/E ratio of 5 ($10/$2 = 5).

Ratios reveal a great deal about a company. When you're looking into them, make sure to keep these two points in mind:

1. A ratio is just one number divided by another, and is certainly less complicated than it seems at first. Think of them as "flags" that indicate areas of strength or weakness.
2. There's no correct value for a ratio. Whether a ratio is too low or too high depends on the overall industry, the company's competitors, the strategy of the company, and your own perspective.

Now, to know that a company's shares trade at $10 does not tell you whether that is a good price. Maybe the stock is worth much more or much less than that and therefore could be either a good buy or a really bad buy.

On the same note, knowing that a company made $2 per share in earnings doesn't tell you whether that's really good or merely lackluster, because it doesn't consider other important factors, like the number of shares outstanding.

So, financial ratios will help you:

- Take numbers in context.
- Directly compare them to competitors.
- Directly compare them to companies of much different sizes.

To stay with our P/E example, by dividing the stock's price by the earnings per share, you suddenly and easily see how strong the company is when compared to its competitors, its industry, and the overall stock market. This is because you can contrast the other P/E ratios directly against our example company's P/E ratio. This takes company size out of the equation so that you can compare a $20 million penny stock directly against a $40 billion blue chip.

Would the $40 billion company have greater earnings than the $20 million penny stock? Certainly, and very much so. Thus, comparing their earnings directly against each other tells you nothing of value, and nothing about which is the better investment, which operates more efficiently, or which has the greater operational success.

Instead you compare P/E ratios of the two companies. You find that the smaller company has a P/E of 9 and the much larger gorilla of a company has a P/E of 18. (Lower P/E numbers are better, by the way!) Suddenly you've revealed, based on the trading price of the shares of each company and their earnings results, that the penny stock company is a much more attractive investment, all other things being equal.

In this example, the smaller company's shares (with a P/E of 9) cost $9 for every $1 of earnings that it produced. The larger company (with a P/E of 18) cost $18 for every $1 of earnings it generated. The $10 million penny stock is generating twice as much in earnings as the blue-chip company for each of your hard-earned dollars you invest in the shares.

Of course, a $40 billion company probably makes greater total earnings, but you'd possibly have to pay $85 (for example) for each share you wanted to buy. Meanwhile, a $20 million company, while making less in total earnings, might only cost $0.65 (for example), so you may be able to buy more earnings power for much less money.

Hopefully you see the power of financial ratios. It levels the playing field so that you can compare companies of all sizes and types and different industry groups with each other, and generate much greater clarity.

Financial ratios also work great when comparing companies of similar sizes within the same industry—especially when you are deciding which of the two (or three or four) to potentially invest in.

Picture two companies (ABC and XYZ) that are similar in every way, except the following (don't worry, you'll learn shortly what each of these ratios tells you):

- *P/E ratio* (lower numbers are stronger): ABC = 71, while XYZ = 32.
- *Debt/equity ratio* (lower numbers are stronger): ABC = 4.0, while XYZ = 0.2.
- *Current ratio* (higher numbers are stronger): ABC = 1.2, while XYZ = 21.0.

In this example, XYZ is the much more attractive investment. This is because you're paying $32 (compared to $71) for each $1 of earnings power. Also consider that:

- XYZ has 20 cents of debt (compared to $4) for each $1 of company equity.
- XYZ has 21 times more current assets (compared to 1.2) than current liabilities.

In fact, ABC is a pretty unattractive company. XYZ seems stronger across the board, based on just these three financial ratios. Is XYZ a better value? Yes. Is XYZ a good stock purchase? Maybe, but you'd still want to do more research to find out. How does XYZ score with the other major financial ratios? How does it compare to the industry average? How does it stack up against the rest of its competitors?

Table 6.5 lists the five operational aspects of any company and the categories of financial ratios that can be applied to them during analysis.

Table 6.6 displays some of the more common financial ratios and what they can tell you about a company. In most cases, you won't need to calculate any of these on your own, because they are freely available through various financial web sites like MSN Money and Yahoo! Finance.

A Special Ratio: Profit Margin

A profit margin is the money the company makes after the cost of producing the product or service. For example, if a company has a product it sells for $10, but it costs the company $8 to make that product, then the profit margin is $2—the difference between the sale price ($10) and the cost of production ($8).

Usually the cost of the product involves the parts needed to build it, the cost of assembling it in the factory, and the cost of shipping it out. All of that adds up, and takes away from the profit the company would have generated.

A company with a 30 percent profit margin is going to be three times as effective as a company with a 10 percent profit margin. The higher the profit margin, the better.

Picture a company that can sell something for $100 that costs it only $50 to make. The competition is also selling the product for $100, but it costs this other company $70 to make it. The first company has a strong advantage. It has a 50 percent profit margin and makes $50 per sale. The competition has a 30 percent profit margin and makes only $30 per sale.

Profit margin is one of the most powerful financial ratios. It reveals how effective a company is in its own operations, but also provides you with an idea of how it stacks up to the competition.

Table 6.5   The Five Aspects of a Company

Financial Ratios provide insight into five aspects of a company:

Liquidity	Can cash and current assets pay all the obligations as they come due?
Activity	Displays the efficiency of the company's operations.
Leverage	Demonstrates the mix of equity to debt.
Performance	How profitable is the company?
Valuation	Are the shares worth the price they are trading at?

Table 6.6   Financial Ratio Cheat Sheet

Financial Ratio:	How it's Calculated:	What It Tells You:

Liquidity Ratios (Current, Quick, Cash, Operating Cash Flow)

Financial Ratio:	How it's Calculated:	What It Tells You:
Current Ratio (Look for at least 1.0, or higher)	$= \dfrac{\text{current assets}}{\text{current liabilities}}$	The ability to pay near-term obligations.
Quick Ratio (look for at least 1.0, or higher)	$= \dfrac{(\text{cash} + \text{accounts receivable} + \text{marketable securities})}{\text{current liabilities}}$	Immediate cash + short term investments available to satisfy short term debt.
Cash Ratio (higher numbers are better)	$= \dfrac{(\text{cash} + \text{marketable securities})}{\text{current liabilities}}$	Ability to pay current debts with cash on hand and liquid securities.
Operating Cash Flow	$= \dfrac{\text{cash flow from operations}}{\text{current liabilities}}$	How many times cash flow generated by operations covers short term obligations.

Activity Ratios (Turnover Calculations for Inventory, Receivables, Payables, Working Capital, Fixed Assets, Total Assets)

(Continued)

Table 6.6 (*Continued*)

Inventory Turnover	=	$$\frac{\text{costs of goods sold}}{\text{Inventory}}$$	How many times their inventory is sold and replaced over time.
Receivables Turnover	=	$$\frac{\text{sales}}{\text{average accounts receivable}}$$	Average numbers of times accounts receivable are collected in a year.
Payables Turnover	=	$$\frac{\text{sales}}{\text{average accounts payable}}$$	The rate at which a company pays off its suppliers.
Working Capital Turnover	=	$$\frac{\text{sales}}{\text{average working capital}}$$	Compares the depletion of capital to the generation of sales over time. How effectively is the company using it's capital?
Fixed Asset Turnover	=	$$\frac{\text{sales}}{\text{average fixed assets}}$$	Reflects the productivity + efficiency of property, plant, and equipment in generating revenue. The higher the ratio, the better the company is at using its fixed assets in business operations.
Total Assets Turnover	=	$$\frac{\text{sales}}{\text{average total assets}}$$	Efficiency in using assets to generate sales.

Leverage Ratios (Debt to Equity, Debt, Interest Coverages)

Debt to Equity	=	$$\frac{\text{total liabilities}}{\text{total stock holder's equity}}$$	Indicates the proportion of equity + debt the company is using to finance its assets.
Debt Ratio	=	$$\frac{\text{total liabilities}}{\text{total assets}}$$	Displays debt as a percentage of assets.

Table 6.6 (*Continued*)

Interest Coverage	$\dfrac{\text{(net income + interest expense + tax expense)}}{\text{interest expense}}$	The ability to meet interest payments.

Performance Ratios (Also called Profitability Ratios)
(Gross Margin, Return on Sales, Return on Assets, Return on Equity)

Gross Marin	$=\dfrac{\text{(sales – cost of good sold)}}{\text{sales}}$	Illustrates the percentage of revenues that remains after the costs of making/ providing the product or service.
Return on Sales (Also called Net Profit Margin)	$=\dfrac{\text{net income}}{\text{sales}}$	Illustrates percentage of net Income generated from and compared to total gross sales. How efficient is the company?
Return on Assets (Also known as ROA)	$=\dfrac{\text{net income}}{\text{average total assets}}$	How profitable is a company relative to assets? ROA displays how efficiently management uses its assets to generate earnings.
Return on Equity (Also known as ROE)	$=\dfrac{\text{net income}}{\text{average stockholder's equity}}$	How much profit does the company generate by using the money shareholders have invested.

Valuation Ratios (Price to Earnings, Price to Sales, Book Values)

Price to Earnings (lower numbers are better than higher)	$=\dfrac{\text{current share price}}{\text{sales per share}}$	How expensive are the shares, based on the company's ability to generate sales?
Book Value per Share	$=\dfrac{\text{assets – (liabilities + preferred stock + intangible assets)}}{\text{number of shares outstanding}}$	Illustrates how much value a company would have per share, if it went out of business. (This is not a useful ratio for most speculative, high growth, or start up penny stocks.)

A 65 percent profit margin is tremendous, and even more telling when the competition has only a 20 percent profit margin, and the industry average is merely at 30 percent. That 65 percent profit margin could indicate that our example company is a very compelling investment.

Trends in Financial Ratios

As discussed earlier, when you look at a penny stock's financial results (income statement, balance sheet, cash flow statement), you then:

- Look for trends from previous results.
- Develop an expectation for future results.
- Compare the results to the competition, industry, and overall market.

Similarly, when you calculate financial ratios (price/earnings, profit margin, etc.), you should:

- Compare to the ratios in previous periods.
- Generate expectations for what the upcoming ratios will look like.
- Compare these to the competition, industry, and overall market.

When you get to this point in Leeds Analysis, it would be very surprising if you didn't naturally have a clear idea of the relative quality of the investments you are researching. Do you have more clarity about which are the more risky or unattractive ones, and which represent the greatest potential value? That clarity will get more focused and certain as you proceed through the next steps in Leeds Analysis.

Experience Level 5
★★★★★

Trading Tactics: Position Sizing

"You eventually lose all that you gamble with."
—Chinese proverb

Position sizing is one of the most important concepts in this book, and within investing in general. I will simplify it as much as possible, since it's a complicated topic.

If you bet 100 percent of your money every time you traded, you eventually would end up broke, even if you were right 99 times out of 100. That's because you put all your money into each trade, and the losing trade would fully wipe you out.

If you bet 50 percent of your money each trade, any losses would be very costly, even if you had a high frequency of winning trades. Even the best traders have a few bad trades in a row, from time to time.

If you're able to make a series of 10 or 15 winning trades without taking a loss, then you certainly don't need this book. Realistically, you'll make your mistakes and you'll have your successes. The idea behind position sizing is to limit the damage you'll incur from those losses.

Position sizing has two facets:

1. Limiting losses when stocks start falling
2. Limiting the percentage of your portfolio invested in any one stock

For example, a position sizing strategy of investing 10 percent of your holdings into 10 different stocks and selling immediately if any of these shares drops more than 10 percent will be very effective at preserving your capital. The most you would lose on any bad trade would be 1 percent of the overall value of your holdings (10% of portfolio, sold at a 10% loss = 1% of total value).

On the other hand, a position sizing strategy of investing 25 percent into 4 stocks and selling if you took a 25 percent loss would be much less effective. On a bad trade you could lose over 6 percent of your total portfolio (25% of portfolio, sold at a 25% loss = 6.25% of total value).

Too often the overall market turns ugly, and even good traders take three or five or eight losses in a row. When this happens, do you want to lose 20 percent of your portfolio or 65 percent? With position sizing you're more likely to live to fight another day.

(Continued)

Trading Tactics: Position Sizing *(Continued)*

In general, if you have a $5,000 portfolio, it might make sense that you invest 5 or 10 percent per stock that you buy. If you have a $20,000 portfolio, it could make sense to invest 3 to 5 percent in any one penny stock that you buy.

Position sizing can be accomplished in terms of:

- Percentage of portfolio per investment
- Dollar value per investment
- Number of shares per investment

Consider an example of position sizing by dollar value. You might decide to invest a maximum of $2,000 per stock, for example, out of a $50,000 portfolio. This will be safer than $5,000 per stock, and you'll be glad you played it safe if you ever make a string of losing trades.

The idea of position sizing is to limit losses, so that any mistake is confined to a small percentage of your total investment dollars. It's one of the most important concepts in investing, and you should make sure to do it well. If you do it properly, you'll be able to make plenty of mistakes without being significantly impacted.

Additional Fundamental Factors

Industry

The industry in which a company is engaged should make a big difference in your analysis. For example, if a cement plant is losing money each year, that's a bad sign, whereas a biotech company taking annual losses is generally expected.

That's why it's important to compare each company directly against other players in the same industry. Depending upon the industry, numbers that look bad may actually turn out to be very strong when contrasted against others. Numbers that perhaps you thought were great may turn out to be much less compelling once you realize that all of the competition actually enjoy much better numbers.

If the average P/E ratio for a company in a certain industry group is 20, you can then get a better idea of whether the stock you are looking into is strong or weak on that basis. The same holds true for every aspect of the financials, and they should all be contrasted against the overall average for the specific industry.

Trends

In the investment game, the goalposts will be continually moving. Over the months and years, you will see changes in:

- The direction of the economy
- The priorities of consumers
- The policies of governments (local/state/nationwide/international)
- Peoples' habits, beliefs, and activities
- The presidential office and the senate

That's just to name a few. The ways in which the rules can and will change are numerous and complex, and while you can sometimes predict trends, most of the shifts will catch us by surprise.

Sometimes a trend takes decades (think changing from oil to solar). Sometimes it happens in an instant (think 9/11 and the instantaneous implications for military, political, financial, and consumer activity).

Now, if you go against a trend, it's like swimming upstream. On the other hand, if you spot a trend early enough and react to it, you're setting yourself up to benefit.

You wouldn't want to buy into a fur coat company if it had become politically incorrect to wear fur. The company's customers, and therefore its revenues, would be dwindling down; soon the shares may be as dead as the minks the company skins. There would also be implications for all aspects of the fur industry, from the hunters all the way down to the advertising companies that had some furriers as big clients.

On the other hand, perhaps a drop in purchases of fur started that resulted in an increase in purchases of leather coats, or expensive jewelry, or fine cars. People have often bought fur coats because they were very expensive and thus served as status symbols. Those same people, when they gave up on fur, would look to other kinds of status symbols. Perhaps it's a type of car, perhaps it's a type of jewelry, or maybe it's even a different kind of coat. If you can predict the result of the shifting trend, then there will usually be opportunities for you as a penny stock investor.

There are four primary trends that can impact your investment analysis and the companies you may be investing in:

1. Social
2. Political
3. Industrial
4. Consumer

In addition to these, there are many secondary trends that could be important and should be considered when doing Leeds Analysis. Some of these include, but are not limited to:

- Military (focus, spending, deployment regions)
- Investor activity
- Religious beliefs
- Medical (treatments)
- Medical (patient knowledge)
- Technology adoption

A few trends of note in recent history include increased use of seatbelts, improving racial tolerance, the invention and widespread use of the Internet, technology to combat crime (e.g., Lowjack to react to car theft), and so on. There are literally thousands of trends taking shape or underway right now, all around you. If you pay special attention to look for such shifts in society, you might spot a trend or two, and from that you could position yourself to profit.

The examples mentioned are some pretty major trends. There are, however, many micro-trends, which often represent some of the greatest opportunities. Consider some of these micro-trends and think of how you could take advantage as an investor if you were aware of them:

- A new kind of ice cream becomes popular.
- Olympics are awarded to be held in Florida.
- Iowa gets an NFL franchise.
- New Mexico drops its corporate tax to zero.
- Crime rates in rural communities increase dramatically.

With each of these micro-trends there would be dozens of resulting opportunities that could lead you to winning penny stocks. There are thousands of micro-trends, and you'll need to look for and discover them yourself. In the meantime, let's take a step back and review the four primary trends.

Social Trends

Social trends are about what people do, and have, and want, what they wear, how often they shop, what types of foods they eat (and don't eat), and so on.

The majority of consumers used to smoke. Now, far fewer smoke, and those numbers continue to slip. This has resulted (gradually over the long term) in less strain on the medical industry, an increase in average life expectancy, and therefore greater profits for insurance companies. It also brought share prices of major cigarette manufacturers down, although they were very deft in shifting their revenues into other businesses and products; even if the Altria Group (ticker symbol MO on the NYSE) stopped selling cigarettes altogether, it would still bring in hundreds of millions from selling beer and lending money.

Political Trends

In the 2008 presidential election, the Democrats won a landslide victory after eight years of Republicans in power. The ideals of the two parties, and therefore the decisions they make and the priorities they hold, are very different. As a result, you can understand that a shift in the government will have many implications. The results for publicly traded stocks can be positive or negative or neutral. Your job as an investor is to look for the results that will come out of shifts in the underlying political situation.

Imagine this fictitious scenario: Candidate A wants to double the homeland security budget. Candidate B wants to cut taxes. If Candidate A gets elected, you may see increased funds for military technology companies, and increased weaponry sales. If Candidate B gets elected, you may see increased sales for consumer discretionary items like electronics and jewelry, as people spend the result of their tax cuts.

Remember that the implications of political trends go both above the U.S. presidential level (think international politics, NAFTA, UN, EU, OPEC, etc.) and below it (think state by state, or even county by county).

Industry Trends

There are industry-specific trends, and at the same time each industry is affected by major countrywide and worldwide trends. For example, a coal producer in the United States may see global coal prices dropping, while at the same time the U.S. government slaps a tax on coal producers as a way to make clean-energy companies more competitive. In this scenario, coal price changes are an international trend, while the new tax represents an industry trend.

Consumer Trends

This is similar to social trends, except it relates more to the actual activities of consumers. For example, are people shopping more, going further to buy items, paying more on average, and asking for refunds less often?

In other words, how are the clients, or shoppers, or consumers changing the way they do things? Then, how does this affect the publicly traded companies in which you may be interested?

Management

Who's steering the ship? This may be the most important aspect of any publicly traded company. A horrible CEO running a great business is likely to fail, while a great CEO running a horrible business is likely to succeed.

It goes beyond the CEO, of course. There are a number of roles in any company, from CFOs to VPs of sales, from directors of marketing to technology officers. You would want to see strength, experience, and effectiveness in all of them.

Here are some considerations when you look into a penny stock's management team:

- **Age/health.** Just like someone that runs for president of the United States, you have the right to know that the management team is likely to remain in their jobs, and will be capable of achieving their responsibilities.
- **History/previous career.** What were they doing before their current position? Was it successful? Why did they leave? Do they have the experience and expertise from previous roles to be effective now?
- **Ethics.** While this is usually not spelled out to shareholders (although sometimes it is), try to get a feel for their ethical responsibility. Are they taking an unfair salary and milking

the company dry? Were they the subject of legal action against them, either in the corporate world or in their personal life? Are they running this company to help customers and/or shareholders, or is it simply to help themselves? It will actually be very simple to get a feel for a manager simply by having a phone conversation, even when that conversation is about things other than corporate values. While ethics might not be as important to some as it is to others, history has shown that the companies with the greatest successes are led by passionate people with great integrity.

- **Warning signs.** There could be any number of warning signs, and they could take just about any form. Are the CEO and CFO married, and both major shareholders? What happens if their relationship goes south? Is the entire board of directors over 70 years old and therefore not in tune with modern technology? Does the new CTO come from a company that has her covered with non-compete and confidentiality agreements that could either leave her stunted in her new role or make her the subject of legal action?
- **Management changes.** Is the management team very new (less than a year in this job)? Has one or more of the key personnel left (or been released) recently, and whom did they find to fill that role, if anyone? Should the CEO be changed, but instead just remains in his role despite unknowingly holding the company back?
- **Connections.** It's always good when a key manager can lean on high-level alliances, connections, and industry players. Sometimes you'll even see a person brought into a company in a key role simply because of the connections he has. For example, if you're trying to sell your homeland security products, it wouldn't hurt to have your board populated by players and former players from the CIA, military, and government.
- **Additional responsibilities.** Often you'll find a CEO who is also the CEO of another company (or two!). Sometimes you'll see a CFO who also runs his own accounting practice

on the side. Maybe you find a key player who is contractually obligated to travel to China for four days every second week, which may really put a damper on his usefulness.

- **Personal life.** Personal life and business life *do* mix, despite people regularly quoting the opposite. When I am thinking about investing in a company, I want to know if the CEO is an alcoholic, or if the COO has a criminal record for fraud. Unfortunately, it's very difficult to learn most of these things, but if you keep your eyes open you might see something subtle that tips you off. Perhaps you meet the CEO in person at an event (which you made a point of attending for just that purpose) or at the annual general meeting, and you smell alcohol on his breath. Perhaps you do a criminal record search on each of the key players. You'll almost never discover anything to be concerned about. However, sometimes you will, and those are the times that pay off by steering you clear of an investment dud.

Risk

There are two types of risk when investing in any publicly traded company: *company risk* (also called *non-systemic* risk) and *market risk* (also called *systemic* risk).

Company risk represents all the factors that may hurt the underlying share price. For example, picture Company X, which has:

- A pending lawsuit against it
- A burn rate (overall cash loss in ongoing operations) of $23,000 per day
- A 101-year-old CEO
- A workforce that is probably going to go on strike soon

These examples all represent company risk, because they are specific to Company X. Any one of them could result in a deterioration of the share price. If the CEO passes away, or the workers go on strike, or the company runs out of money, or it gets embroiled in (and potentially loses) the lawsuit, the company will face some tough times.

Take a look at any potential stock investment, keeping company risk in mind. How many concerning factors do you see in the worst-case scenario? How does that compare to other companies you're also researching? Basically, in how many ways can things go wrong for the company?

Market risk relates to factors that could hurt a company's share price but are not limited to the company in question. Rather, they are factors that would affect the overall industry or the entire stock market.

Picture Company Z, a young technology penny stock. It may be doing better from one month to the next, but a major meltdown in technology stocks as a group will drag Company Z down in sympathy. Then, what if the stock markets start trading lower across the board, month after month? That young technology corporation is suddenly swimming against the current, despite the fact that it is moving in the right direction from a business operations perspective. This is market risk playing out, because the problem is not specific to Company Z. Rather, Company Z is just an innocent bystander.

When performing Leeds Analysis, you should look for any and all company risk and market risk factors. They won't all come to pass, but if you're prepared for the possible eventualities, then you'll react more effectively to them.

As well, getting involved once a risk factor has taken a company down a little, especially when it's due to market risk or trading in sympathy, can be a great way to buy at bargain prices.

Competition

Competition is strangely overlooked in many people's analysis. Investors get excited when they hear about a company working on a cure for cancer, sometimes bidding the shares up to ridiculous valuations; however, they seem to have forgotten that there are hundreds of other companies working on the exact same thing.

There are four aspects to competition:

1. Market share
2. Momentum/trends
3. Barriers to entry
4. Competitive advantages

Market Share

The percentage of sales that a company captures, out of the total sales for the industry, is its market share. If the total market for skipping ropes is $100 million per year, and the company sells $5 million worth, then it has a 5 percent market share.

This is a quick way to gauge relative size between competitors. Over time, it is also the best way to know whether a company is taking away market share from its competition, or losing out over time.

Picture XYZ Corporation, which last year had 25 percent market share for its product. This year it wound up making less money, which seems like a warning sign at first. However, what if you look into it and realize that it now has 55 percent market share? It turns out that the company is stealing business away from its competition at an impressive rate. Perhaps the drop in revenues was due to cutting prices, which may have been part of its strategy to increase its market share. Now that their product has become more widely adopted by their customers the company may be able to ramp prices back up and potentially make greater revenues, driven by its dominating 55 percent market share.

Momentum / Trends

Keep an eye on trends (increasing/decreasing), especially when compared to the competition. You want to look for:

- An increasing overall market
- Improving market share
- Drops in market share among the competition

A 23 percent market share gives you a perspective of a company's competitive size. However, you'd get even more clarity if you knew that two years ago the company's market share was 4 percent, or 95 percent. Then you'd know whether it is gaining or losing ground.

Barriers to Entry

The worst kind of competition is new competition. If a company is working on handling the competitors it already has, the last thing it wants to encounter is a new player throwing itself into the fray.

The higher the barriers to entry, the better for current players in the market. Once established in a product or service niche, a company wants it to be very difficult for any other companies to go after the same customers.

Picture the Big Three automakers. They don't worry that some new startup will come along and take market share away from them, because the barriers to entry are extremely high. Ford, GM, and Chrysler know that their real competitors are the ones that they already have, such as Volvo, Toyota, and Audi.

On the other hand, imagine a web site that sells weight-loss products. The forces keeping others out are almost nonexistent. It doesn't take much to build a web site and peddle weight-loss or nutritional supplements, and there are no FDA, intellectual property, or patent considerations. In fact, competitors can come in the form of workout programs, a new type of diet, exercise equipment, special membership prices at the local gym, and informational web sites.

Thus, you want to avoid companies that are trying to move into a new market that has prohibitive barriers to entry, or that operate in a field with very low barriers to entry.

Look to invest in companies that have already established themselves in niches with very high barriers. For example, a company that makes a drug to treat arthritis is less likely to suffer new competitors than one that designs web sites. (See Table 6.7.)

Keep in mind that barriers to entry can change. Sometimes government regulations make it easier (or harder) for companies to do things, thus removing (or adding) a barrier to entry.

Table 6.7   High and Low Barriers to Entry

High Barriers to Entry	Low Barriers to Entry
Complicated industrial manufacturing (cars, airplanes, construction vehicles)	Low-end manufacturing (shirts, baskets, signs, furniture)
Patent protected processes / technologies/ drugs	Unpatented properties, or products and services that allow room for "knock-offs" and imitators
Highly regulated by government organizations (pharmaceuticals, military contracting, guns and ammunition, cigaretts)	No regulation (family counselors, lawn maintenance, web site design, hair dressing)
High customer loyalty (automobiles, BlackBerrys and iPhones, couriers)	Low customer loyalty (shampoo, restaurants, alchohol)
Limited theater of operations (mining rights, cell phone airwave rights auctioned by government, radio station frequencies)	Unlimited theater of operations (most things sold online, things that ship to customers)

Picture a tax incentive for businesses that develop green energy. This encourages renewable-resource companies by lowering the barrier to entry of financial costs.

Now picture a patented drug that reaches the end of its exclusive patent allowance. Upon the expiration of that patent, the company is instantly subject to an influx of competing generic drugs, as the major barrier to entry has simply vanished.

On the other hand, what if the government suddenly imposed new strict regulations on sales of kids' toys? This would increase the barriers to entry and would actually be a good thing for the current toy manufacturers that come into compliance.

Competitive Advantages

Competitive advantages allow a company to produce its wares for less, sell its product for more, or gain market share with lower effort.

Think of Harley Davidson. Lots of companies sell motorcycles, but people gladly join the waiting list for a new Harley, because that's the only hog they'll ever consider riding. Most people have a very positive perception of the HD brand, and it's the first motorcycle maker that pops into peoples' minds. That's a tremendous competitive advantage. It allows Harley to sell more, charge more, and enjoy word-of-mouth referrals.

How about a company located in India or Mexico? It has a competitive advantage, because it has a less expensive workforce, and if it is selling its wares to Americans and getting paid in U.S. dollars, then it enjoys a benefit that its stateside competitors do not. A cheap workforce is a major competitive advantage.

A strong competitive advantage:

- Results in easier customer acquisition.
- Allows for faster production.
- Enables a company to charge more.
- Enables a company to produce for less.
- Makes life difficult for the competition.

Consider a technology company with a patent for its process in the United States. No other company can produce the same technology, and thus the patent is a tremendous competitive advantage.

You can see strong competitive advantages all around you. What are the competitive advantages for Apple computers? Southwest Airlines? Trump condominiums?

Experience Level 3

Customers

It is best for a company to have a customer base that is:

- Diverse
- Loyal
- Numerous

This insulates the underlying company from shocks, such as the largest client jumping ship or a hot new product stealing away market share.

Often you will see a defense contractor go belly up when its largest (and only) customer (also known as the U.S. government) dumps its contract. On the other hand, if a business has 10,000 clients, it can easily survive the loss of one.

When performing Leeds Analysis, look for a customer base that is:

- Growing in numbers
- Growing in purchase amounts
- Increasing frequency of repeat purchases
- Paying more per order
- Remaining loyal over the years
- Numerous (the more customers the better)

Allies

It's good to have influential friends. Often the success or failure of a company is based on whom it has on its side. A company that makes car bumpers really benefits when two of the board members are high-level executives at General Motors.

Halliburton Company had one board member, Dick Cheney, who later moved on to become the vice president of the United States. That certainly would have been a well-connected ally to have.

Some companies will have strong relationships from which they benefit greatly on an ongoing basis. For example, picture a small gold mining company that has shared development claims with some of the major producers. The company has access to the people, capital, and relationships that it might need to excel.

Look for companies that are surrounded by bigger, solid players in their industry. Take notice and be cautious of those that don't seem to have any helpful high-level relationships.

Trading Tactics:
Scaling In and Scaling Out

Most less experienced traders buy and sell all at once. They have $3,000, they find a stock they like, and they put all $3,000 into that stock. This isn't necessarily a wise trading tactic, and as anyone who knows my story understands, I learned this lesson the hard way when I first started out.

More advanced traders have a more effective strategy. They *scale in and scale out* of their positions. Simply put, the $3,000 in our example would be invested in two or three or even six chunks, and these buys would happen over days, or weeks, or months.

For example, let's say you have $6,000 and want to invest it in ABC Company. Instead of putting $6,000 into the company immediately, you invest only $2,000 at first.

If that stock starts going higher, the $2,000 is in a profit position. If it starts going lower, at least you've saved the loss that the other $4,000 would have taken. At that point, if you still believe in the investment, you could *average down* by buying more shares with the $4,000 that is still on the sidelines.

This strategy has even been employed in turn-of-the-century military tactics. A good general always holds back some of his troops, and can then respond based on the results of the first attack.

By *scaling in*, you stay dynamic and keep your options open. It also buys you time—time to think about the decision you made and maybe rethink what you are doing with the rest of the money. It also allows you to watch as other events occur, while still having the option open to buy more shares.

For example, you might scale in with a buy in February and come back with a secondary purchase in July and a third in September. In between each of these purchases, you have time to assess the situation and see new events that occur with the company, with its competitors, and with the overall market and industry. You will simply be more informed.

It also keeps your money on the sidelines so that you're open to other ideas. For example, say you were going to put $6,000 in ABC company, but instead you decided to scale in, and you held $4,000 back. Then perhaps another opportunity comes to light, or maybe your kid needs braces so you use the money for the orthodontist. The downside to scaling in is that your broker commissions will be higher,

Trading Tactics:
Scaling In and Scaling Out *(Continued)*

but that's not really a big deal since most stockbrokers charge fairly low commissions.

When you're selling shares, you may want to *scale out*. It's not usually a good idea to dump all your shares onto the market all at once, unless you have only a very small position in the company. With thinly traded penny stocks, unloading even 25,000 shares could push the stock price down while you are selling.

A lot of people use the very common and somewhat effective strategy of selling half of a position if their investment doubles. This gives you back your original investment, and then the idea is to let the other half ride. I find it more effective to exit and enter positions in three, four, or even eight different trades, as long as you are doing it with enough money each purchase to make it worthwhile. I usually space these purchases out over months, and sometimes years.

I bought Absolute Software at 80 cents. It scared me by immediately going down to 40 cents, but Leeds Analysis provided clarity on this stock's direction, so I didn't worry. Soon Absolute reversed and within the next two years approached $8 per share. I sold three different chunks around $7 and $8 over a couple of months. Rather than dumping all the shares at once, I proceeded cautiously, and took my profits a piece at a time.

It's also a good idea to scale in or scale out surrounding an event. For example, a company is going to release its financial results and you expect the numbers to be strong. You might want to buy shares with part of your money before the release of the financials. Then you keep part on the sidelines until you see the actual results. At that point you can decide whether you want to put the rest of the money in; or perhaps now you've changed your mind.

Experience Level 3

Intellectual Property

Patents, trademarks, and copyrights all play a role in any company. However, intellectual property (IP) is especially important with smaller penny stock companies, because without legal protections they can be easily pushed around, stolen from, or trampled. On the other hand, a small company with the right patents suddenly becomes a player that can stand up to the competitive market forces and recoup any possible losses.

As well, strong IP rights make the penny stock much more valuable as the underlying technology or information starts to become more significant. In fact, there are several examples of tiny companies with great patents that end up selling the patent itself for more than the entire company was worth.

Just keep in mind that there are a lot of useless patents out there. In fact, many companies will boast about having a patent on some technology, knowing full well that the technology may not be worth patenting or that the patent itself is too narrowly focused to be meaningful or enforceable. So why talk up the patent? Because it sounds good to prospective investors, soothes current shareholders, and scares off potential competitors.

Make sure that any company you follow has a technology (or drug, or system) worth patenting, and that it has proper, rock-solid legal protections on it. To know this for sure is very difficult, and if you have ever looked into intellectual property rights, or tried having a discussion with the U.S. Patent and Trademark Office, you'll know exactly what I mean. The whole topic is very complicated, and there are a lot of gray areas. In fact, expensive and lengthy legal proceedings are very often required just to find out if Company A was infringing on Company B.

However, a good test of the legitimacy of a patent, and the quality of the technology it protects, is when the company uses the patent to legally stop another company, or to sue for damages. In this event, you would know that the technology was worth trying to copy, and that patent lawyers are willing to argue the merits of the IP rights in front of a judge.

Legal Issues

One factor that can derail a penny stock company is a lawsuit. Even the expense of legal proceedings (whether the company is suing or being sued) can be too much to bear for a small company. That's just in terms of the lawyers' costs, let alone if a major judgment goes against the company.

A $50 billion company could easily survive a few dozen lawsuits. A $5 million penny stock cannot. Be careful of those businesses that have current or looming lawsuits, even if they are the ones that are suing. Of course, it's possible that a penny stock will survive a legal battle or two. However, all things being equal, avoid companies with legal issues.

The one exception to this is a penny stock that has a great technology (or drug or system) that is subject to competitor imitation. It is a very wise use of funds and resources to assert its IP rights to legally block the competition. It also speaks to the merits of the technology itself, since the company's competitors think it's worth copying.

Press Releases (Public Relations/Investor Relations)

Especially when dealing with penny stocks, press releases can really throw a company's share price around. The right "just-awarded contract," or high-level customer win, or patent award can cause the share prices to multiply in value.

You want to have public relations (PR) and investor relations (IR) releases on your side. In other words, it's best when a company knows how to promote itself and continues to generate positive investor interest on an ongoing basis. With smaller companies, the management team may need to sing from the rooftops to be noticed, and if this generates buying interest, shareholders will potentially stand to benefit from higher prices.

Look at a company's PR and IR strategy, and see if it:

- Has frequent releases (without overdoing it)
- Has accurate releases (without having to mislead or manipulate to make them effective)
- Gets increased buying activity in its shares with most releases

It seems that some penny stock companies have a business plan that involves sending out releases but doesn't include much else. They don't make money. They don't get new clients. They don't have any real prospects. They just talk about how great they are, how much money they are about to make, and how great their technology is. Stay far away from these types of companies, if they can't benefit from or back up all the things they are talking about. Remember, it's easy to make a great-sounding press release, but they may simply be dumping their shares into the buying interest that they've generated.

In summary, PR and IR releases are very important and are a great tool for small, high-quality companies to get their message out. Just make sure that there is substance behind their words.

CHAPTER 7

Share Structure

SHARES—STARTING FROM THE BEGINNING

Experience Level I ●★★★

Companies raise money through the sale of their shares. They also leverage the shares to acquire other companies and assets. The downside is when they go too far, as so many companies do, and dilute their shares. We'll discuss all of this, but first let's keep it simple and start from the beginning.

Each share represents one unit of ownership of a company. Picture ABC Corporation, worth about $1 million. Now, if it had only 1 share outstanding, that share would likely trade for about $1 million. If there were 10 shares outstanding, those shares would trade for about $100,000 each, so that the total of all the shares together would be approximately $1 million. With 10 million shares out, you'd expect the stock to be trading closer to 10 cents per share (again, for a total worth near $1 million).

In other words, the total value of all the shares is what the entire company is worth. If investors think the company is worth more, then they pay more for shares, thus driving the share price up, and therefore the overall company's value.

The higher the value of the shares:

- The more money a company can raise
- The fewer newly issued shares needed to raise that money
- The more buying power a company has for acquisitions

Picture a company with 10 million outstanding shares. If its stock price increases by $0.50, the company has just had an increase in its value of $5 million. If it is looking to acquire a small company with shares rather than cash, its buying power also has increased by $5 million.

Insider Trades/Insider Holdings

There are two versions of insider trading. One is legal and serves as a good indicator of management's faith in their own company. The other is not legal, and involves taking advantage of information to which average investors have not yet been alerted.

Let's start with the sensational, illegal version of insider trading. A company insider is anyone privy to specialized knowledge. When that knowledge isn't freely available to the investing public, that insider might abuse his position by unfairly profiting from sensitive information.

Think of a company's CFO who's putting together the financial reports for the latest quarter. Before they are released to the public, he knows that the company's revenues have collapsed, so he sells all his shares before that information is released. Once the poor results are made available to everyone, the stock tumbles as investors dump their shares.

The CFO avoided a major stock market loss by selling before the bad news hurt the shares. Unfortunately for him, he may now end up in jail. That is insider trading at its worst, and it's illegal because it violates the fair functioning of the stock market itself.

Often insiders take friends and family down with them. When they spread the information to others before it's public knowledge, and those people act upon it, they've all put themselves at risk of going to jail or paying major penalties and fines.

Abusing a position of privileged information has caused trouble for many famous and/or high-level personalities (Mark Cubin, Martha Stewart, Bobby Brown, etc.), as well as thousands of people you've never heard about.

This illegal form of insider trading is not the version that we'll be discussing any further. There's another role that insider trades play that is not so deceptive, and is certainly not illegal.

Top management and executives of any publicly traded company, as well as a person, organization, or company that owns more than 10 percent of the outstanding shares, are considered insiders.

These insiders must report any transactions they make in the underlying stock. If the CEO is selling, you have the right to know, and it must be reported by her for all to see. If a holding company that owns 12 percent of a company is buying more shares, you have a legal right to know, and the holding company must report the purchases or the intention thereof.

The theory is that insider buying is a positive sign, while insider selling is a negative sign. This has never been proven to be an effective indicator for future stock prices, but when used in conjunction with the full Leeds Analysis approach it can be another important piece of the puzzle.

If a CEO truly believes in his company and is buying more shares, then it may be a positive sign. If the COO is suddenly dumping her shares onto the open market, perhaps that's a bad sign; maybe she knows something that you don't.

By watching insider trades, you can get another level of insight into the management's opinion of the company's future. If board members and top management have done nothing besides accumulate more shares over the past two years, this may demonstrate a commitment and optimistic belief in the direction and prospects of the company.

Just be sure to read into insider buying and selling with a grain of salt. The value of the purchases and sales is important. If insiders bought 150,000 shares five months ago, but the shares then were only 2 cents each, that $3,000 purchase is not really a commitment or statement.

As well, investors almost always put too much stake in insider transactions and the meaning behind them. Sometimes a CEO just needs some money to buy a boat, so she sells $50,000 worth of shares. History also shows us that management are often buying before share prices fall and selling before they increase, making insider trades a reverse or contrarian indicator. Why do management do so poorly at timing their own share purchases and sales? Simply because they aren't that good at predicting which way the share prices are headed. Being a CEO does not make you a stock market genius. Investors that rely on insider trading simply seem to forget this fact.

When I look at insider trading from the perspective of Leeds Analysis, I do not use it as an indicator of the future share price direction. Rather, it complements my findings about management—specifically, it speaks to their level of commitment and optimism.

Institutional Holdings

Often, big chunks of the outstanding shares are owned by other corporations. It may be:

- Competitors, trying to hedge against their own successes and failures by owning a piece of the competition
- Bigger, cash-rich corporations looking for places to invest
- Companies looking to potentially take over the business in question and keeping their fingers in the pie
- Mutual funds and hedge funds that believe the shares will increase in value

Institutional holdings are freely disclosed and you can check them quite easily online with sites like Yahoo! Finance. In general,

Trading Tactics: Volatility Play Investing

Volatility Play investing allows penny stock traders to make money off of the same stock again and again, by buying near or at the *support levels,* and selling near or at the *resistance levels.* (Support and resistance levels are both detailed in Chapter 8, "Technical Analysis"). Some have misunderstood the concept, thinking that any stock can be used as a Volatility Play. They take a penny stock chart and believe that the buy levels should be somewhere near the year low, or perhaps the month low, and that the sell levels coincide with the upper prices the stock has reached. (See Figure 7.1.)

Such a basic way of applying these concepts to penny stocks is sure to be disappointing when it comes time to tally your results.

To appropriately identify a penny stock that would be a potential Volatility Play, you need to follow these steps:

1. **First, look for a penny stock that has excellent volatility.** The difference from its year high to year low needs to be at least 100 percent, but some of the best Volatility Plays we have ever uncovered enjoyed a difference of 300 to 500 percent. This helps ensure a high level of investor speculation and unpredictability in the underlying stock.

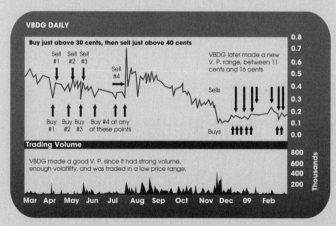

Figure 7.1   VBDG Trading

(Continued)

Trading Tactics: Volatility Play Investing (*Continued*)

This does not mean you will be buying at the year low, and selling at the year high. In fact, once you find a penny stock with a huge difference between the year high and low, you then set about making small 15 and 25 percent profits from it.

2. **There also needs to be a pattern of trend reversals.** The penny stock needs to have hit and tested its lower and upper prices several times, preferably two bottom tests and one or two upper tests.

By testing, we mean that the stock approached its support or resistance level but was not able to break through, and instead reversed direction. The reversal should take the stock most or all of the way back to the opposite test level. For example, if it tests and bounces off the high, it should then drive directly toward the low over the following trading days. (See Figure 7.2.)

3. **The penny stock needs a clearly identifiable support level and excellent strength at that level.** This does not mean that the support level needs to be at a round number, like $1.00. Rather, if a company has just recently announced a stock buy-back plan, you can be assured that it will have a range within which it intends to pick up shares. If you can identify this level through a surge in volume and a rebound from a certain low price, you can expect that there'd be good support at that level.

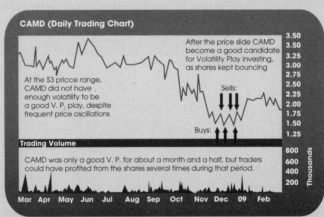

Figure 7.2   CAMD Trading

Trading Tactics: Volatility Play Investing (*Continued*)

While share buyback prices can change over time, many companies do most of their purchasing at a certain level, sometimes just to keep their shares at or above that specific point.

In addition, if buyers seem to dip into the market at a certain level, you can usually identify this through increases in volume and a strong rebound off of the support level, brought about by sudden buying demand.

A good Volatility Play penny stock always has a strong and easily identifiable support level. This may be $0.45 or it may be $1.00, but you should be able to pick it out easily on the chart through a combination of volume and price analysis.

4. **A good Volatility Play will have an obvious price level where traders tend to take profits.** Unlike a support level, which may or may not be at a threshold number (like $1.00), resistance levels are almost always at a threshold number for penny stocks.

   While a penny stock without a resistance level may just keep rising over time, the difficulty is that you won't know when to take your profits. A stock without a clear resistance level could reverse on you at any time.

5. **A potential Volatility Play also needs good daily trading volume.** At the very least, look for penny stocks that see an average of 100,000 shares change hands per day. The more trading activity, the better. In fact, it's almost impossible to properly identify true support and resistance levels on stocks that have low trading volumes.

   Keeping these five guidelines in mind, remember that Volatility Play penny stocks may not hold their pattern for very many cycles, and can break free at any time. You'll benefit more by your ability to pick good Volatility Plays in the first place than you will by trading well.

   Identify several potential Volatility Plays, in fact many more than you'll actually be investing in. This allows you to watch the entire flock and pick your moments. Most Volatility Plays will be in a buying opportunity only about 5 percent of the time. You buy into the ones that approach their support levels while passing on the ones that are not currently reaching your targets.

   (*Continued*)

Trading Tactics: Volatility Play Investing *(Continued)*

Timing

- The best time to buy is right after the penny stock bounces off the support level. This ensures that you get a low price, and that the support will probably hold (as opposed to the shares just nose-diving toward zero).
- The second-best time to buy is right before the stock hits support, but is trading very close to the support price. The problem with this timing is that the penny stock could see the support level fail and the price fall right through to lower levels. Be ready to cash out and take losses in the event the prices drop below the support level.
- The best price to acquire shares is just above the support price. For example, if support is at $1.10, you may want to acquire shares at $1.15 or even $1.12.
- The best time to sell is just before the stock reaches the resistance level. Drops from profit takers can be quick, so it's usually more effective to sell too early than too late.
- The best price to sell is just below the resistance level. For example, a $2.00 resistance is best sold into at $1.95. (Or even $1.85 to be safe, especially if the penny stock has a history of collapsing back very quickly).

When investing in this fashion, make sure to factor in more frequent commission charges from your broker. You'll be trading more, so you'll pay more frequent commissions.

Also, make sure that the range of volatility is enough to support profits. You may be buying and selling in a tight price range of only 15 to 40 percent. If you are making 15 percent profits on a few hundred dollars, you may be merely breaking even after paying trading commissions and taking the occasional loss.

Make sure that the changes in price direction and the degree of price activity are not based on fundamental factors like news releases, changes in financial performance, or other items mentioned in the discussion on fundamental analysis in Chapter 6 of this book. A company may have been a great Volatility Play, but if it gets a huge FDA approval, the trading ranges can get thrown out the window.

Remember that you don't necessarily have to sell all of your shares each cycle. This applies even more so if you're not positive about the upper resistance threshold, or you aren't even sure if the stock will

Trading Tactics: Volatility Play Investing *(Continued)*

follow your volatility expectations. You could sell half or a portion of your position and let the rest ride.

You may benefit by gradually increasing the amount you invest in each cycle. If you have made some profits, have a good feel for the stock, and the support and resistance levels have proven out near the prices you expected, you may want to put more cash onto the table.

A Note about Jumping Ship

If you have pegged a stock's support level at $1.00 and the price breaks below that, you can know that perhaps:

- Your anticipation of the support level was wrong.
- The stock is not a Volatility Play after all, and the concepts presented in this section do not apply.
- Some fundamental or technical factor has arisen that has forced a failure of the support level.

In any of these cases it might be best to liquidate your position as quickly as possible, trying to take only a 5-to-15-percent loss. If you hold every Volatility Play that sinks past your support levels, you'll eventually wind up with a portfolio of sinking ships.

The beauty of Volatility Play investing is that you should be taking frequent profits, so the strategy *allows* for some losses in the interest of the overall picture.

greater institutional holdings, with a greater number of institutions, demonstrate that professional analysts and money managers, and/or industry allies and competitors, believe that the shares represent a good investment. Assuming that these players know what they are doing (and history shows us that sometimes they do and sometimes they don't), then it may speak to the future expectations of the stock.

Dilution

Dilution is when a company issues more shares, thus making the value of each share worth a little bit less. In theory, doubling the number

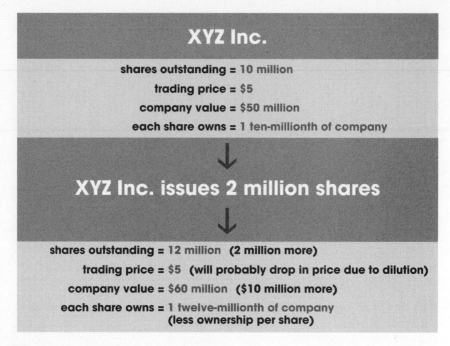

XYZ Inc.

shares outstanding = 10 million

trading price = $5

company value = $50 million

each share owns = 1 ten-millionth of company

↓

XYZ Inc. issues 2 million shares

↓

shares outstanding = 12 million   (2 million more)

trading price = $5   (will probably drop in price due to dilution)

company value = $60 million   ($10 million more)

each share owns = 1 twelve-millionth of company
(less ownership per share)

Figure 7.3   Effects of Share Dilution

of outstanding shares cuts the value of all of the outstanding shares in half. (See Figure 7.3.)

Let's say XYZ Inc. is worth, in total, about $50 million as a company. It has 10 million shares out, which are trading at $5 each. The company wants to raise money for operations, so it issues another 2 million shares, which will trade freely on the open market with the other 10 million.

There are now 12 million shares out, and instead of each holding claim to one 10-millionth of XYZ, each now owns only one 12-millionth of the corporation. Thus, all 12 million shares should be worth a little bit less since there are more shares of the same company. However, by issuing the 2 million new shares, the company may have sold them for around $5 apiece (in our example), thus raising $10 million in cash.

The end result is that the 12 million shares each own a part of a company that has more cash and thus is worth a little more overall. However, there are more shares and more shareholders, so each of their shares holds rights to a little bit less of the corporation.

In the best scenario, the issuance of the additional shares does not hurt current shareholders, but actually helps them by strengthening the company. Unfortunately, in most cases companies are issuing the shares because their business model is burning up cash. If they spit out more shares every time they need to raise money, they will dilute the value of the shares. Such companies, unless they turn things around, often produce endless amounts of shares and tank the value of all of them.

On the other hand, well-run companies sometimes issue shares to raise money and then use that money to advance the company, which eventually makes all the shares worth much more.

Buybacks

This is the opposite of dilution. Often a cash-rich company feels that the market is not fairly valuing the shares, so it buys back stock on the open market. These shares are then retired (meaning they will no longer exist), which makes the value of the remaining shares greater. (See Figure 7.4.)

For example, ABC Holdings has $10 million in cash, with 80 million shares outstanding. Its penny stock is trading at 25 cents, giving the company a market capitalization (total company worth based on the share price) of $20 million. The company feels that it is worth a lot more and therefore should be trading higher. It does not have any plans for usage of its money, and decides that one way to help its share price may be a buyback.

Share buybacks do several things:

- They usually help the share price, since buybacks are often a positive development for shares.

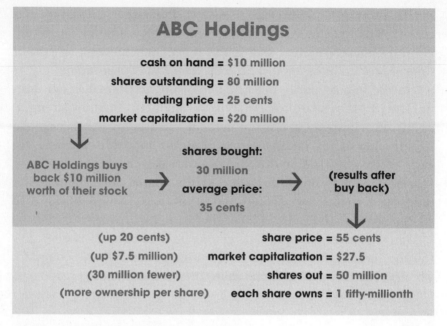

Figure 7.4   Benefits of Share Buybacks

- The trading price of the shares will probably increase as the demand is greater.
- Shares that are purchased get retired, making the value of each of the remaining shares greater.
- They demonstrate a belief by management that shares are undervalued.

ABC Holdings proceeds to purchase and retire $10 million worth of its own stock on the open market over the course of the next 12 months. The company manages to buy 30 million shares at an average price of 35 cents.

The end result might look like this:

- The company has, for example, pushed the share price higher to 55 cents, up from 25 cents.

- The total company value is now closer to $27.5 million, up from $20 million.
- There are now only 50 million shares out, down from 80 million.
- Thirty million shares have been retired.
- Each share owns more of the company (because there are fewer shares).

In general, a stock buyback is helpful for shares and a good indicator that management believes the shares are undervalued.

Acquisitions

Companies often leverage their shares, although they sometimes use cash as well, to acquire another company. Usually it's a much bigger corporation scooping up a smaller one, but this isn't always the case.

The reasons one company may acquire another can be to:

- Get the personnel.
- Have ownership of the patents, technologies, or intellectual property.
- Gain the customer base.
- Gain the brand or name.
- Increase revenues.
- Generate company growth.
- Take them out as a competitor.
- Gain a resource land claim.

In general, being acquired will increase the share price of the company, because the larger company usually needs to pay a premium for the shares. For example, to acquire a company whose stock is trading at $4.25, the bidder may need to pay closer to $6.00 per share to entice current shareholders to give up their investment.

In some cases, the smaller company is open to being acquired. Sometimes it has a good technology or business model, and will really benefit by teaming up with a major, cash-rich player. Think Microsoft scooping up a fledgling technology company and taking it to the bigtime.

Other times, the smaller company does not want to be bought out. This is called a *hostile takeover*. Any company that is publicly traded can be bought out by another entity. As long as the majority of the shareholders vote in favor of the takeover, then it is a done deal.

- The first step in any hostile action is often to take a major ownership position.
- Next, offer remaining shareholders a premium above the current trading price.
- Sometimes the acquiring company may start a "proxy war," where it campaigns to demonstrate to existing shareholders why they should vote in favor of the combination of the companies.
- Sometimes the company would need to increase the price it is bidding for shares to an even higher level above the premium that it has already offered.

When the smaller company does not want to be taken over, or it is not getting a compelling offer price, it will fight the takeover. Some companies even have "poison pills," where any hostile takeover triggers certain defensive events, such as current shareholders being allowed to buy more shares at deeply discounted prices.

Technical Analysis

WELCOME TO TECHNICAL ANALYSIS

**Experience
Level 2**
★ ★ ★ ★ ★   We've learned how to discover the highest quality
penny stock companies using Leeds Analysis. The next step is to get
those companies at the best prices and at the perfect time.

As I mentioned earlier, *technical analysis* (TA) is the examina-
tion of the trading chart in order to (hopefully) predict the direction the stock may take in the future. You can get trading charts at
any of a number of free financial sites, such as Yahoo! Finance or
BigCharts.com.

In general, technical analysis has had varying degrees of success
for investors of all skill levels, and with stocks of all sizes. One of the
major problems of using the past to identify the future is that past
patterns and trends can change at any time.

Until now, TA could not be applied to penny stocks, because the
low trading volumes and small market capitalizations negate many of
the theories. To address this concern, my company has developed our
own TA methodology as part of the overall Leeds Analysis process,
with the specific purpose of applying it to thinly traded penny stocks.

Many of these TA techniques are simple, and even common-
sense, but this is by design. Higher-order TA just does not work with

thinly traded stocks, and certainly not well enough to be trusted. There isn't enough activity to provide certainty or strong probabilities of future price direction.

TA indicators like Bollinger Bands, Fast Stochastics, and RSI are useless when it comes to penny stocks. If you don't know what these are, don't worry, you won't need to. Besides, even if you were a master with these and other TA techniques, they wouldn't help you when it comes to the tiny companies that Leeds Analysis uncovers.

We've enjoyed tremendous success with our TA approach for many years. Over that time we've also refined and fine-tuned the strategy, so that you'll get the greatest advantage.

Look for the following TA patterns and trends in penny stocks, and if you spot them early, you stand to profit.

General Range

By drawing a couple of quick lines on a trading chart, you can usually find a penny stock's *general range*. As you know, this doesn't mean that past performance will be continued. However, sometimes it's possible to see that the shares have bounced mainly between a specific upper and lower price. This general range, while it can change at any time, can serve as a way of knowing what to expect from the underlying penny stock.

Figure 8.1 provides an example of the general range. Note that the company, Forward Industries, uses the ticker symbol FORD. This may cause some confusion for investors who think that they are looking at Ford Motor Company (ticker symbol F).

Figures 8.2 and 8.3 also display the general range of two other penny stocks.

This pattern can be established due to support and resistance levels, or simply as a result of general trading activity. Look for a general range that has remained in place for a while, with increases

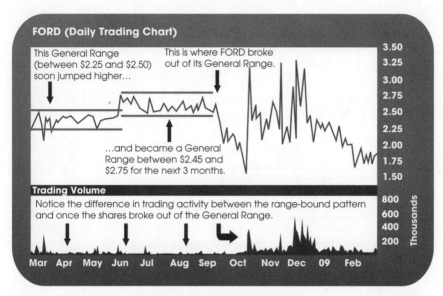

Figure 8.1   FORD Trading Chart—General Range

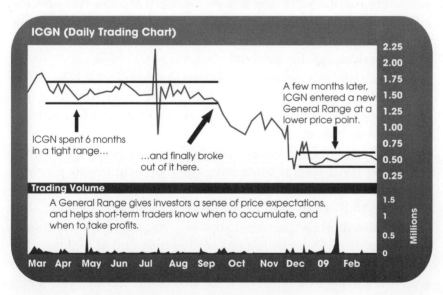

Figure 8.2   ICGN Trading Chart—General Range

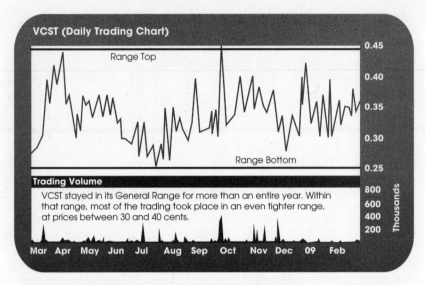

VCST (Daily Trading Chart)

Range Top

Range Bottom

0.45
0.40
0.35
0.30
0.25

Trading Volume

VCST stayed in its General Range for more than an entire year. Within that range, most of the trading took place in an even tighter range, at prices between 30 and 40 cents.

800
600
400
200

Thousands

Mar Apr May Jun Jul Aug Sep Oct Nov Dec 09 Feb

Figure 8.3   VCST Trading Chart—General Range

in trading volume when the shares approach the low end and the high end of that range. Then, you may be able to predict the upper and lower trading prices to expect going forward, at least until the shares break out of that pattern.

If you identify a penny stock's general range, you'll have better clarity about buying and selling decisions. Just make sure to understand that this general range can fail at any time, and be prepared to react to such an event.

For example, if you notice that ABC Inc. has bounced between 20 and 40 cents several times over the past year, it may give you increased confidence to purchase the stock when the shares fall toward 21 to 25 cents (just below the lower end of the range). If it reverses and moves higher after your buy, you might choose an exit point near 35 to 38 cents (just below the upper end of the range).

Have a contingency plan. In our example, let's say you bought at 23 cents. What would you do if the shares then dropped below 20 cents? The general range has been "breached" and is therefore no longer a useful indicator of what the shares might do next.

If you bought ABC Inc. at 23 cents, specifically due to the perceived safety of the lower range price of 20 cents, that reason for buying became invalid once the shares hit 19 cents. At any price below that 20-cent range, you need to reassess your reasons for owning the stock and decide if you should liquidate and take your losses early, since your trading strategy of riding the general range has failed.

Current Trend

Think of a massive ocean tanker—it takes a lot of energy to change direction, or even to slow down. Stocks that are *trending* can be somewhat like the ship in our analogy. While investments can change direction much more quickly, at any point in time they are most likely to keep going in the direction they are currently moving. In other words, any stock has a higher probability of staying on the same course than changing direction.

When a stock is traveling in a certain direction and keeps going in that direction, it is considered to be trending. A trend may be *up*, *down*, or *sideways*.

A typical uptrend may see two up days for each down day. This would result in the stock trading higher from one month to the next, even though it sometimes has days where the price closes lower. The days that see the shares finish higher are more common during the uptrend, which results in the price appreciating over time. This is an oversimplified approach to spotting trends, but by its nature identifying a *current trend* is that easy.

Often, rather than trending, stocks trade erratically. There may be little rhyme or reason to the underlying trading activity, and in these cases using technical analysis to attempt to predict future prices is nearly impossible.

However, other times stocks will trend, meaning that they'll travel in the same general direction for as long as that trend endures. The trend could end today, or not for years. Most trends last months at a time.

The idea is to identify when a stock is trending and to use that knowledge to help you profit. By getting in on a good uptrend early, you could profit significantly and over a long timeframe. You can review Figures 8.4, 8.5, and 8.6 to see some examples of the current trend.

Riding trends is very different from what many investors try to do, which involves "picking the bottom" in price. Trying to buy in at a new low, or guessing the cheapest price the shares will reach, is a very costly and ineffective approach, as is evidenced by the fact that so many investors lose money this way.

Instead, wait until it's clear that the stock has begun a new uptrend. Once you are confident that it's trending higher, you can invest with added confidence because the most likely future direction will see the shares continuing along the same trend. Eventually, this trend will end, and once you get that impression it may be time to jump ship and look for another investment.

You can usually spot a strong trend just by looking at the trading chart. If the line is going higher from week to week, month to month, then the stock is in an uptrend.

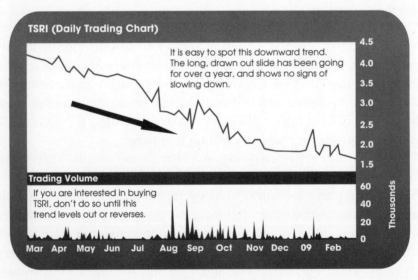

Figure 8.4 TSRI Trading Chart—Current Trend

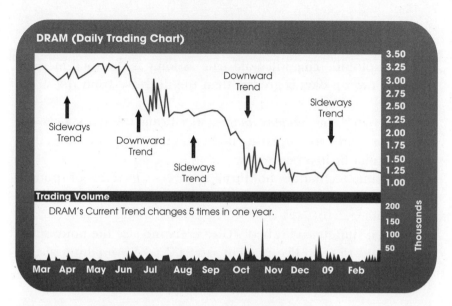

Figure 8.5   DRAM Trading Chart—Current Trend

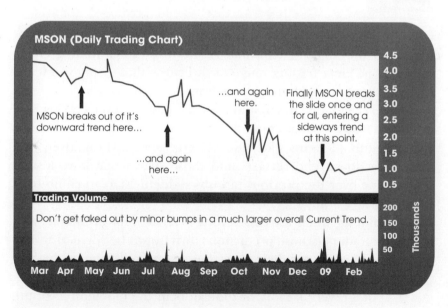

Figure 8.6   MSON Trading Chart—Current Trend

You can also watch the results of each day's trading. If the shares have two up days for every down day, then expect that the stock is in an uptrend. This will hold true as long as the total increase from the two up days is greater than the decrease from the single down day.

Also, watch the *intraday trading*, specifically the day's *highs and lows*. If the shares are displaying higher highs, and higher lows, then the stock may be in an uptrend.

The same techniques hold true in reverse, in terms of spotting a downtrend. Two down days (or more) for each up day would be a downtrend.

Warren Buffett said it best: "Give everyone else the bottom five percent and the top five percent, and I'll take everything else in between."

Trend Reversal

Uptrends and downtrends can drag on for months or years, but eventually they do end. This may result in the stock trading erratically with no clear trading range or direction, thus giving you fewer clues as to potential future price action.

However, it's not uncommon for a trend to reverse. This may result in a stock that has enjoyed a long, sustained uptrend suddenly entering into a lengthy slide toward lower prices. Alternatively, you may see a downtrend reverse, and those shares that have lost so much value over the previous months suddenly start to climb back toward former levels.

Pinpointing when a trend reverses can be very profitable, and it enables traders (whose predictions turn out to be correct) to buy penny stocks very near their lowest prices and sell near the highest prices. (See Figures 8.7, 8.8, and 8.9).

To spot a reversal, look for indicators in the momentum of the stock, as well as the trading activity.

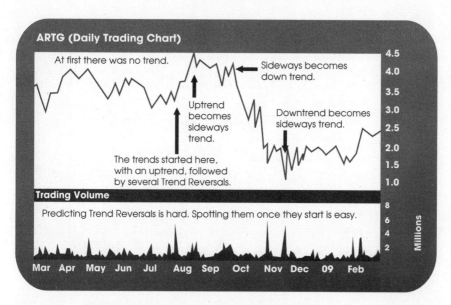

Figure 8.7 ARTG Trading Chart—Trend Reversal

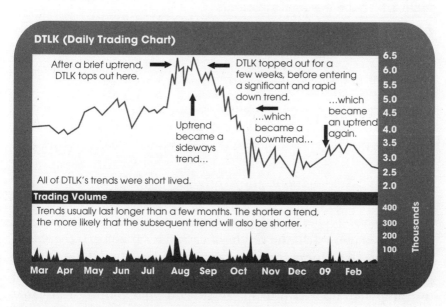

Figure 8.8 DTLK Trading Chart—Trend Reversal

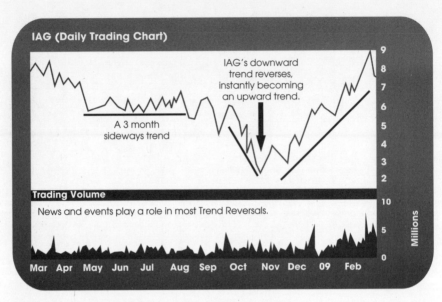

IAG (Daily Trading Chart)

IAG's downward trend reverses, instantly becoming an upward trend.

A 3 month sideways trend

Trading Volume

News and events play a role in most Trend Reversals.

Mar Apr May Jun Jul Aug Sep Oct Nov Dec 09 Feb

Millions

Figure 8.9 IAG Trading Chart—Trend Reversal

Table 8.1 Trend Reversal Indicators

Spotting a Trend Reversal (Fictional company XYZ, Inc.)	Picture XYZ stock that had enjoyed 2 up days for every 1 down day, and with a daily trading volume of 2 million shares.
XYZ's Recent Up Trend:	2 up days for every 1 down day 2 million shares traded per day
Aging of XYZ's Trend:	1 up day for every 1 down day 1.5 million shares traded per day
Reversal Begins:	1 up day for every 2 down days 1 million shares traded per day
XYZ's Down Trend:	1 up day for every 3 down days 2 million shares traded per day

You can also watch the results of each day's trading. If the shares have two up days for every down day, then expect that the stock is in an uptrend, as explained in the earlier section. This is obviously an oversimplified approach to spotting trends, but you will learn that they are quite easy to identify. (See Table 8.1.)

The same techniques hold true in reverse, in terms of spotting a downtrend.

Trend reversals can be a break from an existing trend as mentioned previously. However, the most important trend reversal patterns for penny stock traders are *topping-out* patterns and *bottoming-out* patterns. You'll learn more about these later in this chapter.

Trading Tactics: Trading Windows

Any experienced trader, whether dealing in penny stocks or otherwise, will tell you that the majority of stock gains are produced within short timeframes.

In other words, the big 50 percent and 200 percent price climbs (and collapses, for that matter) often happen in a matter of days or weeks, while the same stock may trade within a narrow range for months at a time, before and after the move.

This is especially true when a penny stock is reacting to significant news. Even the most volatile shares may have a trading range that varies 40 to 100 percent from high to low, but when that news breaks, the price of the shares also breaks out of the range and soars higher (or lower) within a matter of days—or hours!

To make the most of your money, you should try to anticipate the gains that these windows provide, rather than holding the shares over the longer term.

There are four ways that we've identified to increase your chances of holding shares just before they make their moves:

1. Technical Analysis Indicators

As detailed in Chapter 8, some trading patterns help you anticipate a breakout or strong upside price move. Penny stocks often bounce off of *support levels*, *reverse* their trends, explode out of *consolidation patterns*, or *bottom out*. Each of these technical analysis patterns can potentially identify an upcoming penny stock price move.

(Continued)

Trading Tactics: Trading Windows (*Continued*)

2. Type of Company

Different penny stocks are prone to different trading activity depending on the industry or sector they're involved in or the type of business they operate.

For example, retail stores have a certain predictability of earnings and revenues that doesn't allow for sudden explosions of price. Instead, they are more susceptible to longer, less dramatic price trends.

Meanwhile, a biotechnology company can see its share price suddenly double or cut in half based on news, rumors, or even rampant speculation. FDA approval? Lawsuit from side-effects of its primary drug? Even small sparks can ignite (or kill) a biotech penny stock.

Other penny stocks that are subject to spiking higher include:

- Research and development corporations.
- Companies with inventions that require patent approvals.
- Businesses that operate on a contract basis, where one major client or job could represent a significant portion of their total revenues. (For example, defense industry suppliers often see their share price thrown around suddenly, based on government contracts won or lost.)
- Latest "in-the-media" hot stocks. (Some past examples of such industries include nanotech, dot-com and Internet, Bluetooth, uranium mining, and any business poised to conquer the Chinese market.)
- Resource exploration companies (not producers).

Some examples of companies that aren't necessarily subject to the same sudden price moves include:

- Restaurants
- Retail
- Entertainment
- Mining and resource producers (not exploration companies)
- Furniture makers

Most companies, however, fall somewhere in between the examples given here. Such stocks are subject to price moves if the driving forces of their industries suddenly factor in. For example, a war in the Middle East will affect oil production stocks, or a company making clean energy technology suddenly benefits from a new government policy.

Trading Tactics: Trading Windows (*Continued*)

3. Volatility

Some stocks are naturally more volatile than others, for any of a number of reasons. You can get a feel for the propensity the shares have to move simply by looking at a trading chart. What's the difference between the year-high price and year-low price? How many times did the shares change direction, and how quickly did the price ramp up or fall off? How long did major price moves last?

There is a numerical indicator known as *beta* that is simply a calculation of a stock's volatility. You can see the beta for any stock on various financial sites, such as Yahoo! Finance. A company with a beta of 1.0 will be no more or less volatile than the overall market. A beta of 3.0 means the company is three times more volatile than the overall market, while 0.5 would mean that the company is half as volatile. Using beta, you can quickly see what to expect from the activity of the underlying shares.

To get the most out of these volatile penny stocks, try to accumulate at the bottom of the volatility as detailed later in this chapter in the section about "Support Levels." Then the price swings can become your friend, as they send shares higher, and quickly.

4. Anticipation

It is possible to predict the approximate time when most companies will release their financials (or you could just e-mail their public relations contact and ask). If you expect the details to surprise the Street and you get involved before the release, you may be in for a good price ride.

If you can anticipate other types of releases, you may be able to benefit even further. For example, many biotechs will delineate their timeline for product development, FDA applications, expected approvals, and product sales. Sometimes it's just a matter of reviewing their previous annual report.

By having this information ahead of time, you could locate key buying opportunities just before the company has several upcoming landmark dates. If the price is right, load up on shares several weeks before they are expected to finish the development of their latest product. Certainly a news release can be anticipated, and in many cases it will probably affect the stock price, even when it doesn't include any material changes or surprises from the company.

(Continued)

Trading Tactics: Trading Windows (*Continued*)

From another perspective, anticipating the biotech's timeline can help you develop exit opportunities if you are hoping to sell shares and want to liquidate into a potential price pop to get a better profit.

The same concepts can be applied to stocks from different industries. Just be aware of the timelines, potential effect of releases, and expected results.

Just as importantly, be sure to review and apply the Trading Tactic from Chapter 1, entitled "Buy the Rumor, Sell the Fact."

Trading Activity and Volume Considerations

Trading volume can help you identify some of the various technical patterns described in this book, but it's also an excellent technical indicator simply by itself. Current daily volume when compared to previous daily levels, from weeks or months ago, can reveal increases and decreases in trading activity. These changes can tip you off to optimum buying and selling opportunities.

Usually with increases in trading activity, unless it's a major sell-off for fundamental reasons, penny stocks usually benefit. They are exposed to higher interest, and the word is getting out about the company. Penny stocks rarely quadruple in price without an accompanying increase in trading activity. (See Figures 8.10, 8.11, and 8.12).

On the other hand, if volume is drying up, especially if it's approaching almost nonexistent levels, you should be concerned. The underlying penny stock may have fallen out of favor with investors and could see a slow attrition as current shareholders continue to sell into light buying interest.

So, how do you gauge activity levels? What is considered high trading volume, and what is considered low? It all comes down to historical averages. You can use sites like Yahoo! Finance to get the average trading volume for the last 90 days and/or last 12 months.

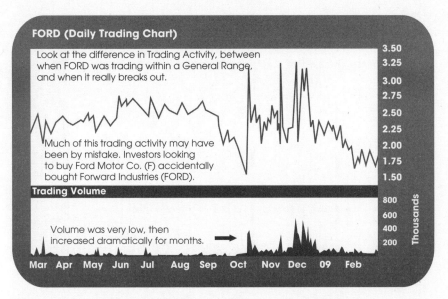

Figure 8.10   FORD Trading Chart—Volume Considerations

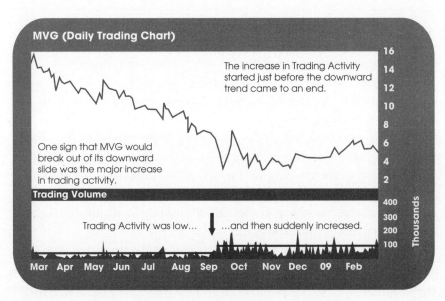

Figure 8.11   MVG Trading Chart—Volume Considerations

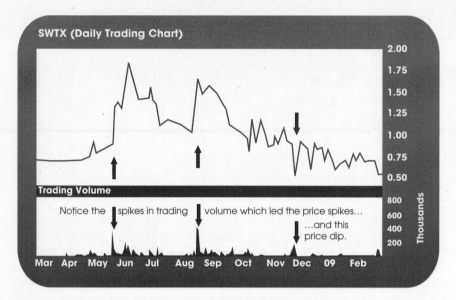

Figure 8.12 SWTX Trading Chart—Volume Considerations

Alternatively, just take a glimpse at the volume bars at the bottom on just about any trading chart.

Is recent trading volume outpacing the averages from the previous month? Is the activity showing signs of slowing down from day to day, or is it picking up?

What does the stock price do during these times? If the shares are falling in value while trading volume increases, you can bet that some major shareholders, or numerous smaller shareholders, are unloading their positions. If the price is rising during increasing trading activity, then you're probably looking at motivated buyers who are gobbling up the shares.

Like anything, with practice you'll quickly find that you can learn about the future direction of a stock simply by observing its trading activity. As you become better at such interpretations, you should see the benefits in your trading results.

Support Levels

Some penny stocks enjoy *support levels*, which are prices the shares are less likely to fall below, due to buying pressure.

Often with penny stocks the support level will form at a threshold price, like $1.00 or $1.50, for example (as opposed to $1.12, or $0.83). This is because many people tell their brokers to "buy at $1.00," or enter their online orders at $1.25, simply because they are nice round numbers.

A support level can also be created when a company is doing a share buyback, and decides that it will acquire its stock at a certain price. The company's buy positions are usually large enough to ensure that its thinly traded stock won't fall below that level.

If this is the case, traders getting in just above the support level (i.e., $1.05 in an example of $1.00 support) are facing limited downside risk while acquiring all the upside potential inherent in the stock. (See Figures 8.13, 8.14, and 8.15.)

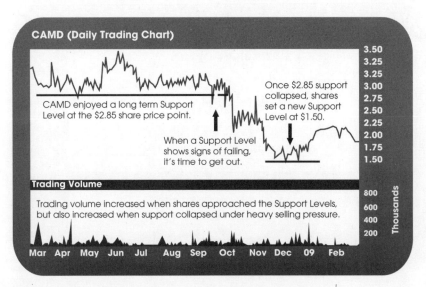

Figure 8.13 CAMD Trading Chart—Support Levels

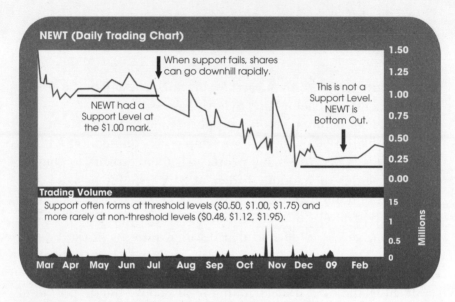

Figure 8.14   NEWT Trading Chart—Support Levels

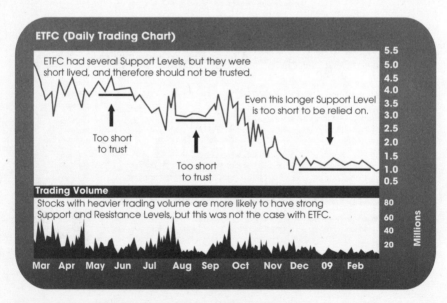

Figure 8.15   ETFC Trading Chart—Support Levels

Often there is a corresponding volume increase whenever shares approach the support. This is because a lot of buyers (creating buying volume) have "gathered" around that certain price, which has therefore created the support.

Remember that while it may potentially increase the chances that a stock remains above the specific price, no support level is immune from failing. When the shares break below a strong support level, the stock may then suffer a precipitous decline.

Also, it's possible for several support levels to exist for one stock. A penny stock may have moderate support at one price, then even greater support at a lower price, and very strong support at a third.

With this technical pattern, an interesting thing can happen. If the stock does finally fall below a very solid support level, that price very often then becomes a resistance level.

For example, if FGH Corporation tests, but remains above, the $2.00 price point, this may be a support level. However, if it eventually falls below that price, then $2.00 very often becomes a new resistance level. It may be very difficult for FGH Corporation to get back above the $2.00 level, and each attempt may see increased selling pressure while the shares fall back strongly. While this isn't always the case, you'll often encounter old support levels that become new resistance levels, and vice versa.

Resistance Levels

This is precisely the opposite of support levels. *Resistance levels* are caused by an increase in selling activity at a certain price, making it difficult for the shares to rise above that level. While the shares can sometimes break through and then move on to higher prices, it's more likely that they will hit that ceiling and then drop back down. For this reason, resistance levels can often be a great point to take profits.

For example, picture a penny stock that keeps approaching $1.00 over a couple of months, but then falls back down each time to lower levels. Each drop-back takes about a week and sees the shares trading near prices close to $0.70. You see an increase in volume each time the stock rises toward the $1.00 mark.

Looking back over the past year, you realize that the shares have never broken above that price, despite four different approaches. Even upon highly positive news and financial reports from the company, the shares still only neared, but didn't break above, that $1.00 resistance level.

In our example, you can assume:

- There is a solid and intact resistance level at $1.
- Very significant positive events will be needed to help the stock break above $1.
- Trading volume will increase as the shares increase toward that $1 level.
- Just below $1 may be a good place to take profits for short-term investors.

See Figures 8.16, 8.17, and 8.18 for some examples of resistance levels. Keep in mind that there can be many different resistance levels for any one stock. For example, XYZ may have difficulty breaking through $1.50 per share. Once in a while, however, sudden buying demand helps break the resistance level and push prices higher, toward $1.80.

It then becomes obvious that there's strong selling pressure at these higher prices, which keeps XYZ from topping $1.80. In fact, as it approaches that level, the selling resistance causes the shares to drop back down below the original $1.50 resistance. Once under $1.50, XYZ may take months or years, as well as many attempts, to ever get back above that point, let alone testing the higher $1.80 resistance.

In many cases, once a trader has identified the support and resistance levels (if any), that trader can profit again and again by accumulating just above the lower threshold and selling just below the upper threshold. I call this *Volatility Play investing*, and detail it in the Trading Tactics feature of Chapter Seven of this book.

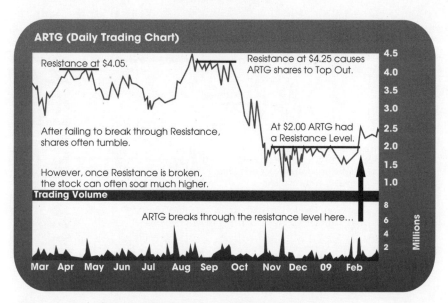

Figure 8.16   ARTG Trading Chart—Resistance Levels

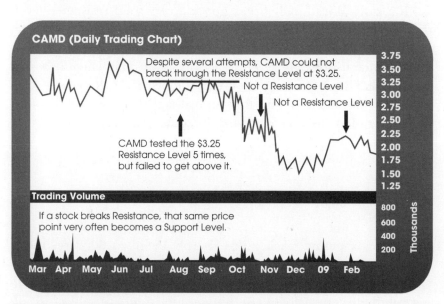

Figure 8.17   CAMD Trading Chart—Resistance Levels

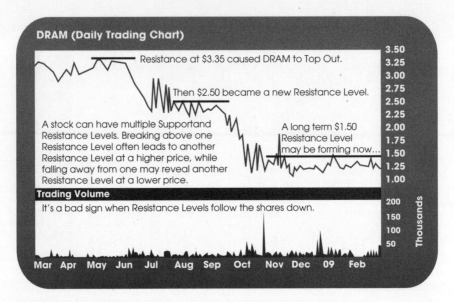

DRAM (Daily Trading Chart)

Resistance at $3.35 caused DRAM to Top Out.

Then $2.50 became a new Resistance Level.

A stock can have multiple Support and Resistance Levels. Breaking above one Resistance Level often leads to another Resistance Level at a higher price, while falling away from one may reveal another Resistance Level at a lower price.

A long term $1.50 Resistance Level may be forming now...

Trading Volume

It's a bad sign when Resistance Levels follow the shares down.

Mar Apr May Jun Jul Aug Sep Oct Nov Dec 09 Feb

Figure 8.18   DRAM Trading Chart—Resistance Levels

If a stock does finally break above a very solid resistance level, that price often becomes a support level. For example, ABC Inc. takes a year to finally break above a longstanding resistance level at $2.50. Once it does, however, that price-point may become a support level. The shares may then trade above $2.50 for many years from that point on. While this isn't always the case, you'll often encounter old resistance levels that become new support levels, and vice versa.

Experience Level 4

Dips

Sometimes a penny stock drops sharply by 10 to 30 percent (or more in some cases), but the dip is based simply on a temporary lack of buying demand (or a sudden increase in the amount of selling volume). Penny stocks are thinly traded, and are subject to suffering *price dips*.

A true dip is temporary in nature, often disappearing with in hours or a couple of days at most, and represents a tremendous buying opportunity. (See Figures 8.19, 8.20, and 8.21.)

If the dip is not based on a deeper problem, it can be an excellent time to accumulate shares. A true dip is temporary, and isn't based on fundamental factors. For example, the share price drops 30 percent on light volume for a day, but there is no reason for the sudden decline besides a sudden and temporary drought of buy orders. Investors who buy into these dips are often looking at profits of 10 to 20 percent within a matter of days or hours.

Generally, the trading volume will be very light at the time of the dip, further solidifying the idea that the price slide was brought on by a lack of activity as opposed to a panicked selloff.

Since they are so unpredictable and short-lived, the way to profit from a dip is to position yourself ahead of time. Having a standing limit order at $0.30 for a stock trading in a range from $0.45 to $0.80 sets you up to benefit any time the underlying stock dips.

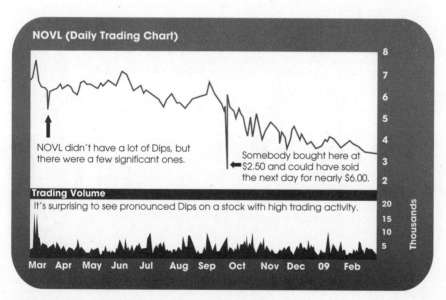

Figure 8.19 NOVL Trading Chart—Price Dips

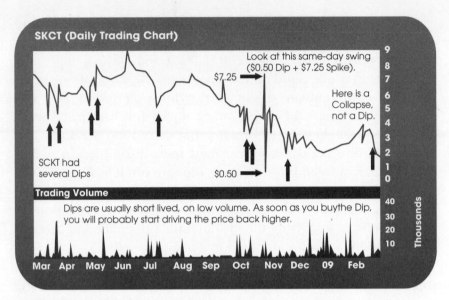

Figure 8.20   SCKT Trading Chart—Price Dips

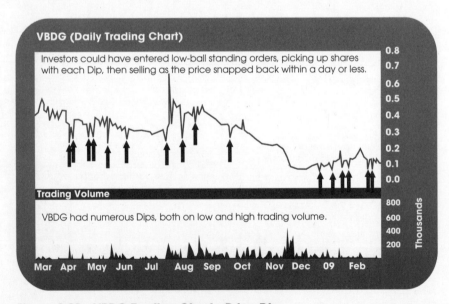

Figure 8.21   VBDG Trading Chart—Price Dips

Some stocks dip more than others, and if you are interested in profiting from this technical pattern, look for those shares that will present you more frequent opportunities.

It's also a good idea to place lowball buy orders on shares of companies that you already own. Picking up some stock at less expensive prices brings your average cost down. However, make sure that the price drop is truly a dip and not a downtrend or a collapse, because in such an event you'd just be picking up more shares as the stock sinks.

Collapse

A *collapse* looks exactly like a dip, except for one major and important difference: The collapse is permanent.

Often this technical pattern is brought on by fundamental factors, such as a lawsuit or a poor financial release. In some cases, however, a penny stock has just been overreaching its true value, and once the buying dries up, there's nothing left to help maintain the prices. (See Figures 8.22, 8.23, and 8.24.)

Usually, investors will be caught off guard. If they had expected a collapse, shares wouldn't have traded so high, and therefore there would have been no need for such a dramatic correction in the stock price.

A typical timeline of a collapse:

- Weakness in the share prices leading up to the collapse (a gradual downtrend, but nothing pronounced yet).
- Sudden and dramatic fall in the stock (often at the market open, but not always).
- Often the fall is so severe that there is a gap between the pre-collapse and post-collapse prices.
- Trading volume is several times the average.
- Following two to five days sees the price drop even further, but more moderately.

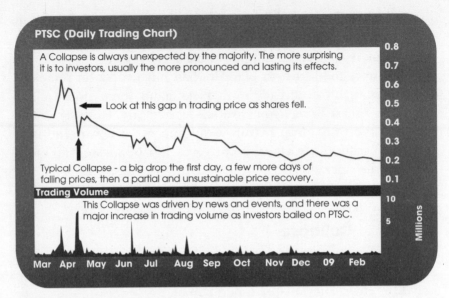

Figure 8.22   PTSC Trading Chart—Collapse

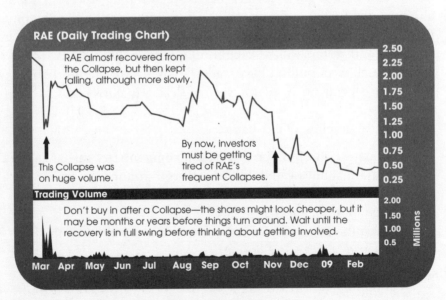

Figure 8.23   RAE Trading Chart—Collapse

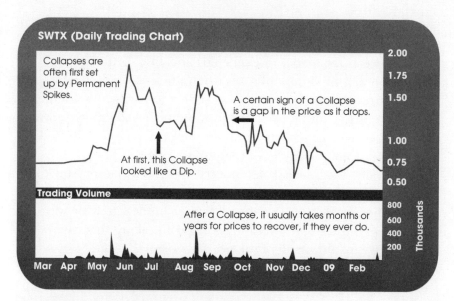

Figure 8.24 SWTX Trading Chart—Collapse

- Volume is still above average on these days, but not as high as the first day.
- Shares regain some of their losses over the course of the next week or so.
- Despite regaining some of the lost ground, the stock then starts heading lower in a gradual downtrend, taking shares toward or even below the lows set by the initial collapse.

You should be able to avoid collapses by getting involved with fundamentally strong penny stocks. If a company has passed Leeds Analysis, it's much less likely that it will collapse, especially since it will have strong valuation ratios and a solid fundamental base.

Temporary Spike

I've seen *temporary spikes* in companies from all different sectors and industries. They are usually fueled by an FDA approval, an appearance at a convention, a major contract win, or any other noteworthy success. Sudden buying pressure sends the stock higher.

The rise is dramatic, unexpected, and fast. Unfortunately, it's also temporary. In almost all cases when the spike is driven by speculation, it quickly deteriorates. This return to earth is by no means as sudden as the initial price explosion, and usually fully unwinds within a few days, or sometimes a few weeks. See Figures 8.25, 8.26, and 8.27 for some examples of temporary spikes.

Generally, with such a temporary spike, the penny stock will see a significant gain on the first day, then lesser gains on each of the next few days. After that point (either immediately or within a couple days), you'll see several days of profit taking that causes the stock to give up almost all of the previous rise.

When you're looking to make a quick profit on the underlying stock, temporary spikes are an excellent exit opportunity. If you're intent on selling out of a position, but you miss your chance with the temporary spike, it may be months or years before the shares return to those levels, if they ever do.

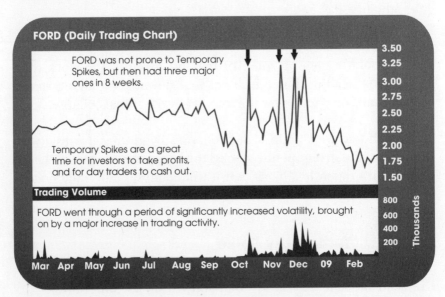

Figure 8.25   FORD Trading Chart—Temporary Spikes

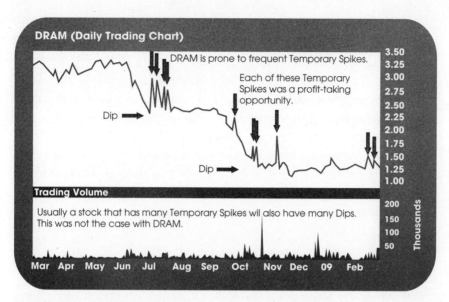

Figure 8.26   DRAM Trading Chart—Temporary Spikes

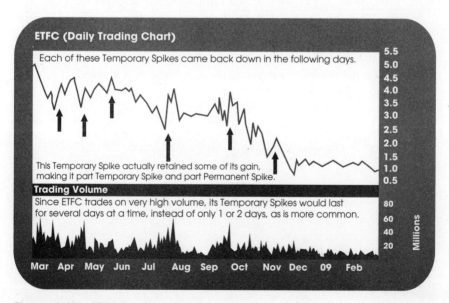

Figure 8.27   ETFC Trading Chart—Temporary Spikes

Temporary spikes are often identified by surges in daily trading volume. By using the trading volume as an indicator, it will help you understand whether the spike is going to be temporary or lasting. If daily trading volume is near its average while the share price increases, it's more likely to be a sustainable move. If the daily trading volume is significantly above the average, the price increase is less likely to be permanent. This is because excessive (stampede) buying often causes share prices to significantly outpace their real worth. The inevitable result is for the stock to readjust back to lower prices once the stampede comes to an end.

A typical temporary spike will follow a pattern similar to the following:

- First, the daily trading volume more than triples its previous average. With that you see the share prices spike dramatically higher.
- Next, the share price moves even higher on the second, third, and possibly the fourth day after the initial spike. Each of these increases is progressively smaller than the one before. Along with this slowing price momentum, the daily trading volume dries up.
- For the next several days after the temporary spike, on even lower volume, the stock starts dropping in price, sometimes gradually, other times significantly.
- The end result is a share price near where it started.

Experience Level 4

Trading Tactics: When to Sell

Knowing when to sell is one of the most overlooked aspects of investing. I'm a believer that you set up your future profit or loss when you buy (by getting in at a great price). However, I understand that the sell decision can really have a major impact on the results of the trade.

I once sold too early (in hindsight) with a stock that had gone up in value over 10 times. I scaled out over a few months, and was very happy with my returns, until the stock took off even higher, and fast.

Trading Tactics: When to Sell (*Continued*)

Making a six-figure profit is great, but it hurts to see that you exited before you would have realized a seven-figure gain!

A number of factors come into play when making that final sell decision. Of course, if you scale out over time, or dollar cost average your position on exit (both concepts are explained in this book), you won't be quite as stressed out about the decision.

Now remember, we're dealing in penny stocks. We use Leeds Analysis to uncover companies that we expect to multiply many times over in price. Less experienced traders seem to forget this, as they cash out for 50 percent and 100 percent gains, only to see the shares keep on ramping up. For a 25-cent stock to go to $5.00, and absolutely change your life, it first has to go to 50 cents, then 75 cents, then $1.00, and so on. You can rest assured that there will be investors gladly taking their profits each step of the way, only to miss out on the big score.

The other end of the spectrum involves being greedy, and not taking a good profit when it presents itself. You're up 100 percent, but wait to see if it could go even higher. Then, as the shares drop back to earth, you kick yourself, wondering why you didn't cash out.

So how do you know when to sell, and when to hang on? How do you know when you should exit a losing position and take losses? There are a few indicators you can use that may be of help.

When deciding whether to sell, consider:

- Whether you have a potentially more profitable opportunity for the money
- Your risk tolerance (is it too high with this stock?)
- Your stress level (don't keep stocks that make you lose sleep!)
- Whether you need the money for something else
- Whether it's the best use of those funds
- Whether you've reached an original goal (e.g., to double your money)

Assuming you are in a position to either hold or sell, the right move may become clearer by considering the following:

- **Trading activity.** Refer to the "Trading Activity and Volume Considerations" section earlier in this chapter. Spikes and dropoffs in volume will give you clues as to whether a climbing price is

(Continued)

Trading Tactics: When to Sell (*Continued*)

running out of steam, or a trend is reversing, or shares are poised for a big jump.

- **Technical trend.** Refer to the sections "Current Trend," "Trend Reversal," "Resistance Levels," "Support Levels," and "Topping Out" in this chapter. Each of these provides you with clues to understand what is happening with the share price, and what to expect going forward.
- **Original reasoning.** Why did you buy the shares in the first place? Do those reasons still apply? Have the company's prospects improved or declined? If the penny stock is executing well on its business plan, then it may make more sense to have patience. If many things have changed since you originally got involved, you should revisit the idea of owning the shares.

Consider this: If you just found out about this company today, would you buy into it at these prices? Even better, forget everything you know about the company, and perform Leeds Analysis from square one. Put the company through the Leeds Analysis ringer, looking for both warning signs and opportunities.

Of course, it often makes sense for those that are still unsure to scale out part of their position. This locks in some profits, but also keeps you involved in a penny stock that is on the way up. In the case of a falling stock, you take part of the loss but the rest remains invested to potentially take advantage of a recovery in the share prices.

Permanent Spike

When a fundamental factor, such as a new contract win, drives the stock price higher, it may cause a *permanent spike*. At first, these look a lot like temporary spikes, but they don't give back the price gains. They also take place over a longer timeframe, and the move usually occurs in a less dramatic fashion, and with less trading volume, than a temporary spike.

A permanent spike can send a stock 50 or 100 percent higher in a day, but sometimes it happens more gradually, and often takes place in 10 and 30 percent moves over the course of a few weeks. (See Figures 8.28, 8.29, and 8.30.)

With very quick increases in price, it's usually based on obvious reasons, such as an announcement of increased earnings, or a press release revealing that the company has landed a major contract.

When the cause of the price increase isn't so obvious, you may see the spike form over the course of a week or two. When this happens, it may simply represent an increase in valuation by investors, and might not be based on any specific event or press release.

It is important for investors to recognize the difference between temporary and permanent spikes. A temporary spike may represent a great and momentary profit-taking opportunity. On the other hand, it may be a mistake to sell your shares if it turns out to be a permanent spike, since the prices have increased on a fundamental basis, and there could be even more upside and little downside from this new level.

There are a few simple ways to tell the difference, although these guidelines are certainly not always applicable.

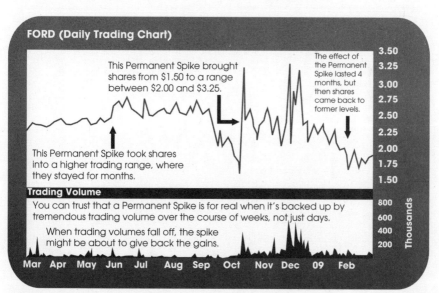

Figure 8.28 FORD Trading Chart—Permanent Spikes

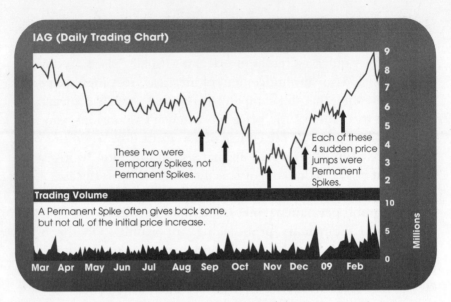

Figure 8.29   IAG Trading Chart—Permanent Spikes

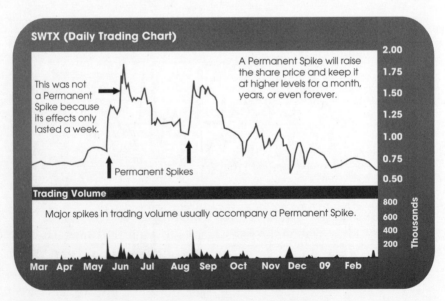

Figure 8.30   SWTX Trading Chart—Permanent Spikes

The following is true of temporary spikes:

- They have a sudden and significant volume increase.
- The volume drops off quickly in the following days.
- There's a major increase in share prices (50 percent to several hundred percent).
- The speed of the price increase lessens dramatically in each subsequent day.
- They last from one to four days, but usually about three.
- They often have a corresponding press release, but not one that will have a long-term impact.

The following is true of permanent spikes:

- Further gradual price increases from day to day.
- Gradual increases in trading volume.
- The trading volume remains high for weeks.
- They have minor increases in price on any given day.
- Minor price increases add up to result in a major price advance overall.
- They last indefinitely and may be followed up by another permanent spike taking shares to an even higher level.

Topping Out

After a steep or long-term rise, shares may begin to trade flat, giving the look of a plateau on a mountain top. This may be a *topping-out* pattern, caused by an increase in profit takers who are selling shares, while at the same time the buying interest begins to dry up.

As the daily trading mix goes from being driven by buyers to driven by sellers, the penny stock begins to trade sideways. Then as the last buyers disappear, the stock begins to fall. Figures 8.31, 8.32, and 8.33 each display a topping-out pattern.

This downward slide wakes up all the other profit takers that had been on the sidelines, who now begin to worry they are missing

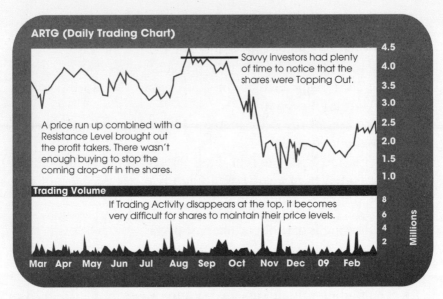

Figure 8.31   ARTG Trading Chart—Topping Out

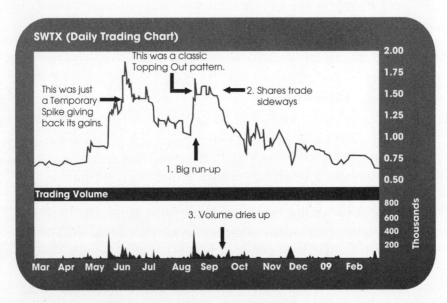

Figure 8.32   SWTX Trading Chart—Topping Out

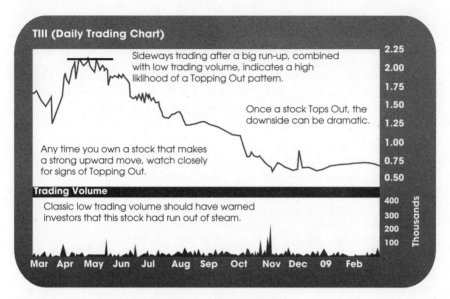

TIII (Daily Trading Chart)

Sideways trading after a big run-up, combined with low trading volume, indicates a high liklihood of a Topping Out pattern.

Once a stock Tops Out, the downside can be dramatic.

Any time you own a stock that makes a strong upward move, watch closely for signs of Topping Out.

Trading Volume

Classic low trading volume should have warned investors that this stock had run out of steam.

Figure 8.33   TIII Trading Chart—Topping Out

the boat to cash out. The further down the shares go, the greater the momentum of the slide.

Often the rise before the topping-out pattern, as well as the fall after, can take as much as six months each. The topping-out pattern that occurs in between will last for a few weeks, or possibly a few months.

If you enjoyed a runup in your penny stock and that momentum is losing steam, you may want to start preparing to exit some or all of your position. If you then witness what looks to be a topping-out pattern, you should be even more sure that the shares may start heading lower.

Be careful with this assumption, however. Many times a penny stock will top out simply because it has risen so far, and so fast, and is simply "taking a breather" before ramping up on another uptrend. Pay attention to the signs of topping-out patterns to make sure that you know whether the stock is due for a fall or is just getting ready to go even higher. (See Table 8.2.)

Table 8.2   Identifying Topping-Out Patterns

TOPPING OUT OR PREPARING FOR ANOTHER RUN UP?

Topping Out patterns warn that the stock is coming back down in price. Be careful, however, because stocks that have been performing well often look like they are Topping Out, only to "take a breather" before soaring to new heights.

Topping Out:	Preparing to Trade Higher:
Daily volume drops off significantly, compared to previous weeks and months	Trading volume remains stable, at average or above average levels
Price trades flat, or slightly lower, after a previous up trend	Prices trade flat after previous up trend
News and events that were price drivers during the previous up trend have started to become more rare	The company still has frequent news releases, and upcoming events that shareholders are looking forward to
Other companies in the overall industry are Topping Out together	This company is bucking the industry trend, and has traded stronger than competitors in recent months
Stock experiences 1 or 2 down days for each 1 up day	Stock experiences 1 down day for each 1 or 2 up days

Bottoming Out

This is the opposite of the topping-out pattern we discussed earlier. Instead of shares falling off after a big rise, this pattern involves a stock price that stabilizes after a lengthy slide and then slowly turns back into a positive uptrend.

Bottoming out usually lasts for many months, and the pattern almost always takes far longer to play out than a typical topping-out scenario. This is because investors are wading back into a stock that has just had a long, protracted decline in share price, and they are understandably wary. They buy in slowly, and with small purchases, and it takes a long time for this buying pressure to stabilize the shares and subsequently to start pushing them to higher levels. Figures 8.34, 8.35, and 8.36 demonstrate bottoming-out patterns.

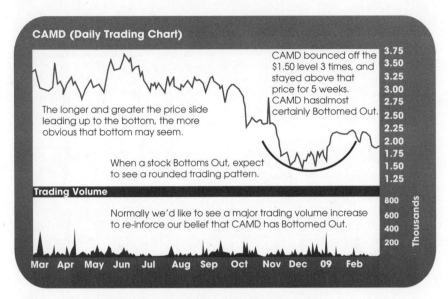

Figure 8.34   CAMD Trading Chart—Bottoming Out

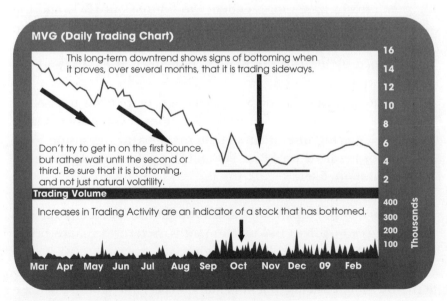

Figure 8.35   MVG Trading Chart—Bottoming Out

177

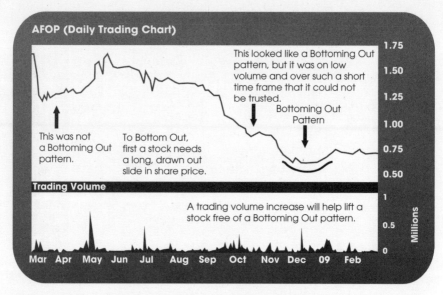

AFOP (Daily Trading Chart)

This looked like a Bottoming Out pattern, but it was on low volume and over such a short time frame that it could not be trusted.

Bottoming Out Pattern

This was not a Bottoming Out pattern.

To Bottom Out, first a stock needs a long, drawn out slide in share price.

Trading Volume

A trading volume increase will help lift a stock free of a Bottoming Out pattern.

Mar Apr May Jun Jul Aug Sep Oct Nov Dec 09 Feb

Figure 8.36 AFOP Trading Chart—Bottoming Out

Some stocks have more tendency to bottom out (BO) and top out (TO), while others never display these patterns. It's all due to the types and numbers of investors, the number of shares outstanding, the activity level of the traders, fundamental events, and the business type.

Any penny stock that does bottom out is more likely to also top out after a large rise, and vice versa. Therefore, if you suspect shares might be entering one of these patterns, look to the history over the previous year or two. Past TO and BO patterns make another such event more likely.

When you notice a bottoming-out pattern, make sure to have the patience to let it play out before you buy in. There may be several bounces in price, and many months, before the share prices actually start moving significantly higher.

Make sure to keep an eye on trading activity. With a true BO pattern, you should usually (but not always) expect a significant increase in daily trading volume. This will add weight to the theory that the shares are bottoming, because it displays an increase in traders buying in at these lower prices. When the buyers are moving back in, the stock is highly likely to stabilize and subsequently move higher.

Be aware, however, if there is no increase in trading volume. A share price that has suffered a long slide, and then looks to be bottoming devoid of increased buying and selling activity, is more likely a "dead duck." By this I mean that the stock may simply be flat-lining, or preparing for another down leg toward lower prices.

By accurately spotting a bottoming-out pattern, and getting involved just as the shares start coming out of it, you have an opportunity to buy at the perfect time. Generally, over the course of the year following a BO pattern, shares in penny stocks increase well over 100 percent in value.

Consolidation

When a penny stock trades in a relatively flat range for weeks or months, this may be a *consolidation pattern*. Consolidations can happen at any point, and often appear after long runups. They are excellent buying opportunities.

They are a result of shareholders who are impatient or disenchanted with their investment and who are unloading their stock. This subdues the effect of any buyers who are just getting involved for the first time. The end result is an unusually flat trading range.

Think of it as, "Out with the old, in with the new." Current investors are leaving, passing off shares to new incoming investors, with the end result being little price change from either selling pressure or buying demand. The ownership of the company's shares undergoes a major turnover, but the stock looks like it is practically asleep. Review Figures 8.37, 8.38, and 8.39 to see graphs displaying consolidation patterns.

The longer the consolidation pattern, the better. What you want is to see a good turnover in shareholders with a major portion of the company being held by fresh investors.

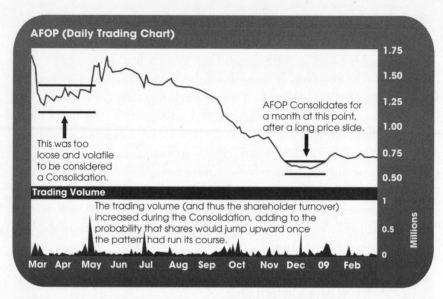

Figure 8.37   AFOP Trading Chart—Consolidation Patterns

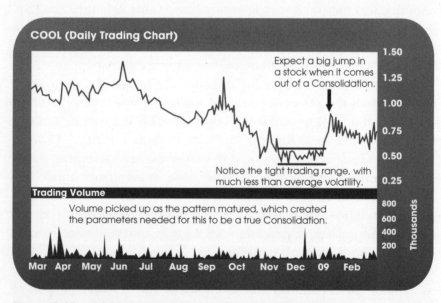

Figure 8.38   COOL Trading Chart—Consolidation Patterns

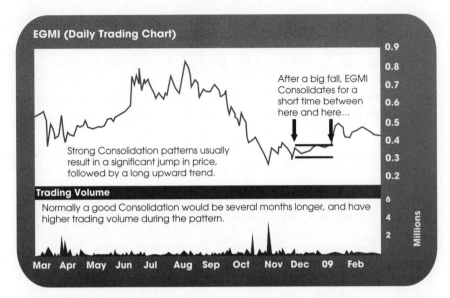

Figure 8.39 EGMI Trading Chart—Consolidation Patterns

If most shareholders have just acquired their stock, they are far less likely to turn around and sell. In addition, if most of the long-term shareholders have exited their position, the upward trend that follows may be unbridled since there are few long-term traders left who would sell into any potential gains.

If you think you've found a consolidation pattern, you can be more sure by doing a quick check of the daily trading volume for the period in question. Add up the number of shares that traded hands the entire time, based on each day's volume. Next, compare that total amount to the number of outstanding shares. This will give you a percentage of total shares that have changed hands.

If there had been a share turnover of at least 25 percent, but hopefully even more than 60 percent, then you may have a strong consolidation pattern. Make sure that the shares traded in a flat or narrow range during that time.

For example, picture ABC Inc., which usually trades with high volatility. It suddenly enters a three-month period where the shares stay in a narrow range, with all trades falling within $1.10 and $1.25. The daily volume for all the days in that three-month period adds up to represent 40 percent of the total of outstanding shares.

In this example, you can be pretty sure that you are witnessing a consolidation pattern. ABC Inc. may be poised for a pretty strong run-up, which could come soon, or perhaps a few months later. Either way, you have increased your odds of making a winning trade.

CONCLUSION

The Way of Penny Stocks

Penny stocks are big business, even though they sound small. Tens of millions of people trade them, and while some win and some lose, none can argue the place of small stocks on the markets.

The broad appeal of these small shares is also notable. Unlike most other investment vehicles that cater to very select niche audiences, people from all walks of life are getting involved with penny stocks. Whether you're a beginner learning the ropes or an experienced trader looking to get in early on tomorrow's up-and-coming corporations, you'll find that others just like you are already involved in the smallest stocks.

Of course, the rules for penny stocks are a little different from other investment types. There are certain risks and pitfalls that could cost you. Thankfully, most of these are easily avoidable, especially if you've read *Invest in Penny Stocks* in its entirety.

You can protect yourself even more by performing Leeds Analysis on any penny stock you're interested in, and by applying the same research to that company's competitors for comparison purposes.

Hopefully, the tactics detailed in this book will get you over the "penny stock phobia" from which most investors suffer. This fear is born of the financial losses that people have taken when they got involved in small stocks because they bought the wrong stocks at the wrong times and for the wrong reasons.

In contrast to this, while dumb decisions and phobias keep some investors out of the penny stock arena, there are many who've been playing the game right. They're the ones investing in the right stocks at the right times and for the right reasons. They're the ones using Leeds Analysis to research their options. They're the ones making fortunes by trading penny stocks.

The good news is that you can get started easily. If you've read through this entire book, then you've been introduced to all the concepts needed to become a successful penny stock investor. From paper trading to getting a good broker, from the best markets to due diligence, you've covered it all.

Most importantly, you've been introduced to Leeds Analysis. By applying it to investments that you may be interested in, you'll be significantly ahead of other investors. You'll avoid those common pitfalls that take some traders out of the game, and profit from tremendous companies as they grow and conquer their markets.

By understanding some of the concepts we detailed in Chapter 5, "Third Level Analysis," you'll spot good brands and shy away from bad ones, you'll clearly see the positioning strategies of the underlying companies, and you'll recognize the need for differentiation. The result will be a unique awareness of the situations of various corporations and an ability to know which will be more effective than others.

Delving into a company from a fundamental analysis perspective tells even more. First, there's the financials, which reveal the fiscal health and momentum of a corporation, from both past and present perspectives. Then, you can get even more granular and review the financial ratios, which allow very valuable comparisons to other companies of all sizes and produce many very telling results.

Yet fundamental analysis goes even deeper. From reading press releases to reviewing legal battles, from researching the share structure to looking into insider trading, you can learn almost everything there is to know about a company. You'll get an understanding of how it fares compared to its competition and develop a pretty good idea of how it will perform operationally.

Of course, finding a great company doesn't guarantee success. You need to know when and at what price to buy shares, and that's where technical analysis comes in. The common trading patterns we've revealed and discussed in this book will round out your Leeds Analysis efforts nicely by showing you buying and selling opportunities that the majority of investors will miss.

Overall, by using Leeds Analysis in combination with your own due diligence, you should be able to find the right penny stocks and buy them for the right reasons and at the right time. You'll get a good entry price and have clarity about the investment while you own it. This puts you well ahead of the majority of investors and should enable you to make significant profits on an ongoing basis, just like a Penny Stock Professional!

Acknowledgments

To the entire Peter Leeds team,

Please accept my gratitude for your outstanding commitment to our collective cause. This book is the result of your efforts and the next step on the path built by your successes.

Everything we've accomplished, and all the triumphs yet to come, are forged by each of us playing our part. Our team has created a grand footprint. Thank you for letting me be a part of it all.

About the Author

Peter Leeds started trading at 14 years old, investing $3,600 into a single penny stock. Within two weeks, he had lost every penny!

Instead of letting his mistakes defeat him, he spent years developing a system that made that money back hundreds of times over. Called *Leeds Analysis*, it helps investors sidestep the pitfalls while finding truly high-quality penny stocks that can multiply their money.

With the success of Leeds Analysis, Peter Leeds has been interviewed by top media organizations like NBC, CBS, CNNfn, Fox, and the Associated Press.

Along with his full team, he publishes *Peter Leeds Penny Stocks*, one of the most popular financial newsletters in North America. Over 32,000 subscriptions have been sold to customers on six continents and from countries all over the world.

He has been a guest speaker for the American Stock Exchange, and has led the panel at Manhattan's prestigious Arch Investment Conferences.

Peter Leeds is the founder of the *100 Percent Unbiased Guarantee*. He and his team take no compensation of any kind from the penny stocks they review. Their commitment to ethics and integrity leads the industry.

> "Ninety-five percent of penny stocks do not pass Leeds Analysis. The 5% that do are far more likely to multiply in value and turn a small investment into a small fortune."
>
> —Peter Leeds

Get More from Peter Leeds!

Subscribe to the *Peter Leeds Penny Stocks* newsletter and start benefiting within minutes!

The online newsletter is instantly accessible, and comes with:

- Penny stock picks
- Daily updates
- Buy and sell price opinions
- The Quick Start Package
- Full company reports

You'll also have access to the Quick Fix—10 stocks that are Undervalued, Undiscovered, and Under $1.

All subscriptions also come with the Peter Leeds archives (going back two years), the Peter Leeds blog, and an extensive bonus article section:

- Learn how to paper trade for risk-free investing.
- Benefit from the Penny Stock Tip Sheet.
- Discover the difference between the investment hyenas and the lions.

Take advantage of our special trial offer today! Get *Peter Leeds Penny Stocks* FREE for two weeks. If you're not satisfied, cancel any time and owe nothing.

Remember! All Peter Leeds penny stock picks come with his *100 Percent Unbiased Guarantee.* Peter and his team take no compensation of any kind from the companies they profile, and they have zero vested interest. All research is done with your best interests as the priority.

Get started now for free, with no risk!

For instant access to your 14-day free trial, visit us online: www.PeterLeeds.com

Index

Index

Index

Index